HERBS

With love and heartfelt thanks
to our parents, who
made it all possible

HERBS

Their Care and Cultivation

SIMON AND JUDITH HOPKINSON

PHOTOGRAPHS BY DENI BOWN

CASSELL

Cassell Publishers Limited
Artillery House, Artillery Row
London SW1P 1RT

Text © Simon and Judith Hopkinson 1990

Photographs © Deni Bown 1990

First published 1990

British Library Cataloguing in Publication Data
Hopkinson, Simon
Herbs.
1. Herbs, Cultivation
I. Title, Simon   II. Hopkinson, Judith   III. Brown, Deni
635´.7

ISBN 0-304-31970-8

Produced by Justin Knowles Publishing Group
9 Colleton Crescent, Exeter EX2 4BY

Editor: Roy Gasson
Line illustrations: Ethan Danielson

Typeset by Keyspools Ltd
Printed and bound in Hong Kong

CONTENTS

LIST OF PLATES

FOREWORD

One of the most marked developments in gardening over recent years has been the revival of interest in herb-growing. One reason for this may be a desire to indulge in more adventurous cooking after encountering exciting dishes when travelling abroad, but another is certainly the realization that many of the plants in a traditional herb garden are extremely decorative in their own right. Herb gardens tend, too, to have an ordered and formal setting, which renders them attractive to people wishing to make striking and satisfying effects in the smaller gardens that are becoming the norm today.

Many people might claim to have pioneered this fragrant renaissance, but few would deny that the work of Simon and Judith Hopkinson in making several medal-winning gardens at the Chelsea Flower Show over the past decade has given the movement a tremendous boost. Their work has demonstrated just how pretty herb gardens can be and given several million people the opportunity of admiring the quality of the plants they displayed and the charming and sophisticated ways in which they framed them.

Even a few minutes' chat with the Hopkinsons can be an enlivening and fruitful experience. Now readers are afforded hours of similar pleasure. This book is long overdue and certain to bring joy. I wish it well.

GRAHAM ROSE

INTRODUCTION

Our interest in herbs started during holidays in the south of France, where we found fresh basil, thyme, and parsley for sale in great bundles in the market in Menton, rosemary, fennel, and myrtle growing wild on the hillsides around, and winter savory, thyme, and lavender thriving among the rocks high in the Alps. Eating herbs became part of our everyday life, and led to our growing them, first for ourselves and, eventually, commercially.

In the early days we received invaluable help from Deni Bown, who introduced us to many of the fine plants which are beautifully illustrated in this book and kindled our growing interest in using herbs more imaginatively and extensively – in the garden as ornamental plants and in combination plantings, as well as in the kitchen.

Among the plethora of books on herbs written in the 1980s, there are few that concentrate – as this one does – on the garden forms of the plants, and fewer still that have such a high proportion of beautiful colour photographs to accompany the plant profiles. It has been a great challenge to decide on our favourite herbs – those that merit their place as plants to grow in a garden. This is a purely personal choice of some of the most attractive and useful herbs in what is an almost unending list.

This book is not an herbal; it offers very little advice on the medicinal uses of herbs. Its two themes are the value of the plants in the garden and, where applicable, their culinary uses. It is for those who have been bitten by the herb bug, and who want to know more about which herbs to grow.

HERBS IN THE TWENTIETH CENTURY

During the early part of this century, herbs were used far more in continental Europe than in Britain. You would probably have found twenty different culinary herbs in common use in France to perhaps one or two in Britain. In 1917, 'Country Housewife', in an article in the magazine *Home Chat*, wondered 'why ordinary people have so few herbs in their kitchen gardens. One sees them in masses in large gardens because really good cooks insist on fresh herbs for flavouring. But in France you rarely see even the smallest garden without a good number of herbs in it.'

During the 1920s herbs, though, began to take on a larger role in people's lives. Britain's first professionally run herb shop – named Culpeper House, after Nicolas Culpeper the 17th-century herbalist – was opened in 1922. It was the first modern shop to sell pure, organically grown herbs alongside herbal medicines and pot-pourris. At around the same time, Miss Gertrude Jeykll was designing gardens for the rich and influential in which her use of herbs was extensive. Although her designs were not strictly *herb* gardens she introduced people to the idea of using herbs as garden plants. Much later, Margery Fish also used many herbs in her garden designs for their scent and form.

The influence of the pen was great in the 1930s – Vita Sackville-West, Margery Fish, Eleanour Sinclair Rohde, and Gertrude Jeykll all wrote books and articles extolling the virtues of herbs in the garden. The year 1931 saw the publication of this century's most important book on herbs, Maud Grieve's *A Modern Herbal* – a comprehensive two-volume work covering thousands of British and American herbs. Although now a little dated, it remains an important reference book.

'Herbs and herb gardens have become a considerable cult during the last twenty years or so' Eleanour Sinclair Rohde wrote in 1936, in her book *Herbs and Herb Gardening*. She was by this time starting to design and plant gardens, mainly of formal design, incorporating a wide range of herbs – orach, chicory, elecampane, hyssop, horehound, meadowsweet, and woad, to name only a few. It was also at this time that the Herb Society of America was founded in response to a growing interest in herbs throughout the United States.

In 1939 Claire Loewenfeld started to investigate the use of herbs in medicine, which led to research and work on special diets on behalf of London's Great Ormond Street Hospital for Sick Children. The medicines were flavoured with herbs to make them more palatable for the children, which led to a need for good, fresh herbs in the winter months. As these were almost unobtainable and dried herbs lacked taste and visual appeal, she decided to grow the herbs herself and experimented with drying them at home. This she perfected and she and her husband eventually set up Chiltern Herb Farms, a company which specialized in high-quality dried herbs for the kitchen.

By the 1950s the acreage allocated to the cultivation of parsley, sage, mint, and thyme – the four main culinary herbs in England – was once again probably as great as it had ever been, most of the production coming from small growers and market gardeners. Some of the crop was set aside for drying, some was used in the preparation of foods such as sausages and stuffings, but large quantities of herbs were used in the manufacture of mint sauce, horse-radish sauce, and tarragon vinegar.

After the war people once more began to travel and to eat foreign food. Elizabeth David played an important part in introducing herbs to the British public through her many books and articles written in the 1950s and 1960s. Her tantalizing recipes, essentially from the Mediterranean regions, always included the local herbs – basil, thyme, sorrel, tarragon, and chervil. Nevertheless, despite this increasing awareness, it was still very difficult to buy any herbs other than parsley, sage, and mint from the local garden shop or nursery.

In 1949 The Herb Farm, founded in southeast England by Dorothy Hewer in 1926, but now under Margaret Brownlow, exhibited at London's Chelsea Flower Show for the first time. It continued to exhibit regularly throughout the 1950s and 1960s. The exhibits, set among displays devoted to new varieties of more specialist and exotic plants, excited much interest. Small herb farms were established in several English counties – Barbara Keen started hers in Shropshire in 1932, while Madge Hooper set up business in Stoke Lacy, Herefordshire. In 1969 one of the first large-scale herb nurseries was started by Barbara Joseph to supply plants to the garden centres that were springing up all over the country. From the basic mints, parsley, and thyme to more exotic rosemaries, sages, and basil, she helped make herbs available to the general public.

Throughout the 1970s herbs became more and more fashionable – journalists wrote about their uses, herb gardens were displayed at the Chelsea Flower Show, and people began to realize that herbs could make attractive garden plants. Herb farms cropped up everywhere, some only lasting for weeks, some still in business and thriving. Culpeper shops opened in most of Britain's large towns. The people of the 1980s fully accepted herbs in all their various guises, and today, it seems, herbs are definitely here to stay.

2

HERB GARDENS

Designing a herb garden is no more difficult than planning any other kind of garden; it is deciding which plants to use that can be much more of a problem. Today's accepted definition of a herb is 'a plant with a use other than that of ornament in the garden'. Botanically this may not be strictly accurate, but the botanical definition, 'a non-woody plant that dies down in the winter', would omit many of the prime culinary herbs such as bay, rosemary, and sage and so reduce the options enormously. Nothing will be achieved by creating a garden using very rigid rules about what should or should not be planted, if the end result is not pleasing.

Our thinking about herbs needs to become more flexible. The over-pedantic herb gardener may reject plants such as male or royal fern, hellebore, and wintergreen on the grounds that they cannot strictly be defined as herbs, but all have a valid place in the herb garden. People are still a little unsure about consciously using herbs as garden plants since the enormous range of plant material that can be classed as a herb is still not fully appreciated. Herbs may be trees – a good example is *Juniperus communis*, whose berries have a wide range of uses in cooking; shrubs – rosemary, sage, witch hazel, and southernwood; climbers – hops, jasmines, and, of course, ivy; roses – the apothecary's and Rosa Mundi; herbaceous plants that die down in winter – lovage, bergamot, and the mints; ground-cover plants – dwarf comfrey, wintergreen, or bugle; evergreen plants – box, yew, germander, and savory; and alpines – thymes, sedums, thrift (*Armeria maritima*),

and catsfoot (*Antennaria dioica*). Although it obviously helps to have a broad definition of what a herb is, you will never find two books that agree on a definitive list.

Even though herbs can be used in any situation, most people buy them for their ornamental or culinary use, filling in spaces in an existing garden. However, with the expanding interest in herbs, more people are prepared to set aside an area for a formal or informal herb garden, or plan and plant a simple herb border. Where the herb garden is essentially for ornamental purposes, with perhaps a small culinary use, it is important to remember that it does not have to conform to any particular style or pattern to be a success.

The first task is to decide whether the preferred site will be suitable for growing herbs. Generally speaking, a north-facing site is difficult and should be avoided wherever possible. This is because many of the herbs likely to be chosen will be of Mediterranean origin, needing warmth and sunlight. South and west aspects will probably give the best results, but partial shade should be no problem, and in some instances might even be helpful. It is always sensible to take note of accepted guidelines, but there are no guaranteed rules for success and it is often simply a case of trial and error. Even though there will be times when your experiments fail, there will be others when you will be happily surprised. Weather always plays a vital part – no two summers or winters are ever the same and each season always brings a new set of circumstances from which to learn. This year's success may be next year's failure but, obviously, the longer a plant has to become established, the greater its chance of survival in drought or a hard winter.

The other factor in choosing a site for your herb garden is the soil. In general, herbs are relatively unfussy, but most prefer slightly acid, lighter soils and the Mediterranean herbs, such as thyme, rosemary, and lavender, need very good drainage. This should not present a major problem – the simple answer is to incorporate plenty of peat into the soil at the time of planting, which will help create a more suitable environment.

Herbs in the Garden

Herbs are essentially uncomplicated plants; many of them seed themselves easily and prolifically, others have roots that can run at frightening speeds if not contained. Nevertheless, some tender annuals, such as basil, are very difficult to grow outside except in the warmest, driest places. Herbs tend to be informal, natural plants that create a soft 'cottagey' feel, especially when allowed to grow unconfined and left slightly wild. Some of the most loved culinary herbs have little to recommend them visually, particularly if they are to be cropped frequently, so might be best planted in a corner of the kitchen garden and treated as a vegetable. Of course, these days, many people have no designated vegetable plot, in which case a small bed outside the kitchen door would be practical, though not necessarily beautiful. For those with no garden at all, a window-box or tub can be invaluable for a supply of fresh herbs.

Using herbs to spot-fill spaces in herbaceous borders or shrubberies can be very successful. A large clump of chives allowed to flower, a tall red fennel with soft, coppery foliage, a lofty queen of the meadow with its dark pink flowers covered with butterflies, or a ginger mint grown in an urn are just a few possibilities.

If you are looking for some new and original plant ideas it is well worth paying a visit to a reputable herb nursery in the summer and seeing for yourself just how stunning some of these plants are and how suitable they could be for so many situations. However, you may be prepared to be more ambitious, a complete herb garden offers an amazing diversity, in colour and fragrance and layout, from the completely formal parterre or knot garden, to a chequerboard or wheel, an informal border outside the back door, or an herbaceous border or thyme lawn.

Formal Herb Gardens

A formal herb design within an existing garden is almost certainly going to be an aesthetic feature that does not necessarily have a practical use, so the location will probably depend upon a suitable site already in mind, which will complement the overall design of the garden. The proportions, of course, are totally arbitrary, but as most gardens today are comparatively small, it seems sensible to make the herb garden comparatively small too, so that it is in proportion to its surroundings.

Formality falls into two broad categories. The first is the design planted largely with classic hedging herbs, probably box, cotton lavender, and germander or maybe hyssop, lavender, and winter savory, with the beds thus created filled in with other, softer herbs. You might decide to plant only the hedges and infill with gravel, using urns and pots to give height and structure, or the hedges could cross each other and make a pattern or knot. The hedged garden will take several years to reach maturity; during the first couple of years the plants must regularly be clipped and shaped to ensure a bushy and even growth. Herb hedges can take many different forms and it is quite possible to mix two varieties of herb in one hedge. Rosemary and lavender, for example, work well when planted alternately, both having much the same growing habit, with the rosemary flowering in spring and the lavender in summer. Another type of hedge could be made by planting a row of green santolina at 18in (50cm) centres and shaping each individual plant into a half-round, so the finished result is like a row of beads touching each other.

The second type of layout, again formal in shape, would depend upon a hard landscape for the outline. The paths and walkways would make a rigid framework, with the individual beds being planted less formally, using a wide range of herbs. This garden begins to take shape immediately the structure is in place; once planted it will take on an air of maturity within the first season.

15

A large, brick-paved herb garden.

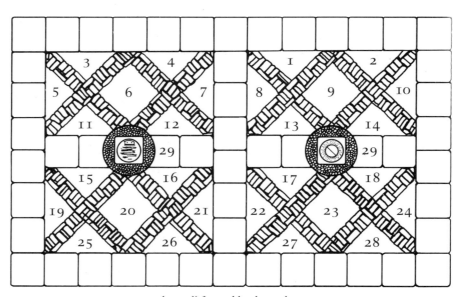

A small formal herb garden.

1 pennyroyal. 2 compact marjoram. 3 pinks. 4 ginger mint. 5 'Silver Posie' thyme. 6, 9, 20, 23 box, with bay in centre.

7 pink lavender. 8 blue lavender. 10 variegated lemon balm. 11 yellow sage. 12 mace. 13 sorrel. 14 cotton lavender.

15 mint. 16 golden marjoram. 17 French tarragon. 18 purple sage. 19 alpine strawberry. 21 blue lavender. 22 white

lavender. 24 dwarf hyssop. 25 white savory. 26 chives. 27 thyme. 28 pineapple mint. 29 sundial bird bath underplanted with thyme.

Informal Herb Gardens

Using herbs informally is much more fun than it seems at first. It is possible to plant herbs in a wide range of styles, from a wild garden, where the herbs are allowed to grow naturally, to a tidy border that to all intents and purposes is an herbaceous border. Certain herbs can be used to great effect by mass planting – chamomile or thyme for a low-growing walkway or lawn, angelica and fennel for a tall informal swathe, rosemary and lavender as a mixed hedge. At Kew Gardens it is possible to see incredible summer bedding-out displays using herbs – red fennel for height, purple basil as an edging, parsley used as a border plant, and various salvias for their flower colour. The added bonus when using herbs in the garden is their wonderful scents and their attraction to bees, butterflies, and other insects.

One of the biggest problems with some herbs is their tendency to reach their peak early in the summer. By the end of July, angelica, lovage, and elecampane have flowered and are setting seed, with their foliage becoming very scruffy. However, others, such as teasels and woad, have the bonus of a fine display of seed heads to follow. It is also unfortunate that some of the finest herbs are annuals or frost-tender, but their advantage often lies in their late flowering, which may well last until Christmas if the autumn is mild. Scented geraniums, salvias, borage, and marigolds all grow more beautiful with time until cut back by the first really heavy frosts. The most effective herb borders will often include a range of tender plants, annuals, and perennials, the latter making the backbone of the garden with the annuals and more tender plants being used to fill gaps and provide late colour.

Herb Garden Designs

A Formal Culinary Herb Garden

This is a practical design (see page 16) for a small herb garden. It could find its place within a medium-sized garden or might, with a little adaptation, make a complete small front garden. The design is flexible, in that it is quite possible to cut the design in half or even, in a very confined space, to use only a quarter of the design. The paving-block and brick paths are useful for containing the spreading herbs, while at the same time allowing easy access.

The size of the herb garden is, of course, determined by the size of the paving stones used. The most appropriate stones would be 18 × 18in (45 × 45cm), although it is possible to use 24 × 24in (60 × 60cm). Using the 18in (45cm) stones, with bricks making up the crosses, the overall size of the garden would be some 20ft × 12ft6in (6 × 3.75m). The bricks should be laid three bricks in one direction with a fourth across the left side; the next section would be reversed, with the fourth brick across the right side, and so on. Please note that house bricks are quite unsuitable for garden use as frosts will soon break up the surfaces. For stability, it is sensible to lay both the bricks and paving stones on a mortar mix, preferably one that is not too wet. Remember that the planting pockets need to give room for the herbs to grow and flourish, so don't bank up the sides of the paths too much; in any case it is not difficult to cut away excess cement the following day. The centre circles in each half of the garden can be built using either bricks or stones set into cement. In both cases it is a good idea to leave a number of holes in which to plant thyme, chamomile, pennyroyal, or other creeping herbs.

The second design is a variation on the same theme – the main differences being that the garden is square and that the hard landscape is built entirely of bricks. This garden is surrounded by a small, ground-level retaining wall, three bricks wide, with the main access paths across the centre. The finished size is to some extent adjustable, but the design works best when built as an 18ft (5.5m) square with the paths about 2ft (60cm) wide; a sundial or urn in the centre would add an elegant finishing touch to the garden. The planting pockets are proportionally larger, which allows each bed to be surrounded with dwarf box hedging, *Buxus sempervirens* 'Suffruticosa', and then filled with herbs. Alternatively, each bed could be planted with several varieties of herbs, thus creating an informal effect within a formal framework.

A Formal Ornamental Herb Garden

This is an uncomplicated garden based on a subdivided square, with four corner beds and a centre circular bed. Being a very versatile shape, it will fit into most gardens and of course can be made larger

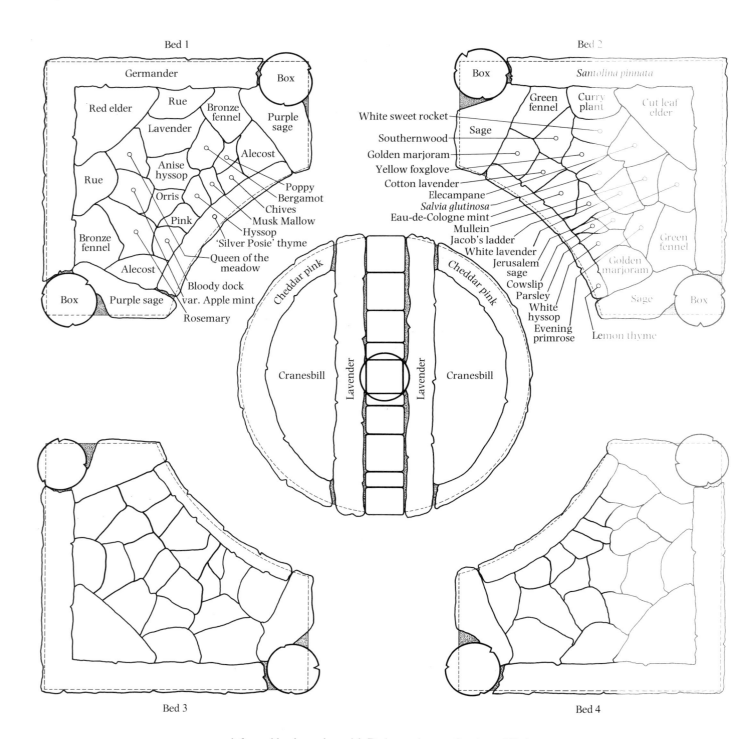

A formal herb garden with Bed 3 a mirror reflection of Bed 2
and Bed 4 a mirror reflection of Bed 1.

or smaller to fit an existing plot. An ideal design for siting in a lawn, this herb garden would be very inexpensive to construct – apart from a few paving stones across the middle of the centre bed, it would just be a matter of marking out the area and cutting out the turf.

This garden has been designed to be placed in a fairly large lawn, the overall size is 35ft (11m) square. The four pathways leading into the centre are of a good width allowing plenty of space to enter the centre area which has a 4ft (1.3m) wide path. The proportions of this garden work well with the plants used – elecampanes, queen of the meadow and elders will all grow to 10ft (3.5m) or more – if the design were to be reduced in size, smaller growing herbs should be used in the centre of the corner beds.

Keeping the lawn edges clipped and tidy is often a problem if plants are allowed to flop over the edge; herbs especially are prone to creep. For this reason and to contrast with the grass, each bed is bordered with a small informal hedge. This adds to the formal lines of the garden making a clear distinction between the green of the herbs and the surrounding grass. Inside the hedges the herbs are informally planted to give a good display of colours and textures over the year. The opposite corners are a mirror reflection of the others.

The centre bed is more simply planted, with a paved path through the middle, and perhaps a sundial or bird-bath placed on the centre stone. Either side of the path is a lavender hedge, which is the tallest growing plant in the central area. The cheddar pinks make a half-moon hedge around the bed which is filled with cranesbill – both plants are very low growing and thus encourage the feeling of being enclosed within the garden, while surrounded by the taller growing and less formal plantings of the outer beds.

A Formal Border

The formal border can be of any length, but is shown here as 25ft (8m) long by 7ft (2.3m) wide, this is really the minimum size needed to achieve the geometric effect. The light grey of the santolina, contrasts well with the large, soft green, flat leaves of the lady's mantle and looks wonderful without being over fussy in shape or content. The standard pyra-

canthas in each diamond give the border necessary height and these are surrounded by catmint. It would work well near a dark hedge, as a border to a drive, or in any situation where a formal planted feature is required.

Once established this type of border requires little maintenance – the lady's mantle and catmint virtually cover the ground. It will be necessary to clip the cotton lavender, which should be informally cut to shape, ideally with a rounded top. The best way to achieve this is to cut the plants hard back each spring after the last frosts, any flowers which start to form should be cut off at once. The catmint and lady's mantle are herbaceous and need all the old material cutting off in the spring. The pyracantha has a strange growing habit and tends to put out shoots at odd angles which will quickly lead to the head becoming misshapen if not removed, otherwise trim as the shape dictates between May and July.

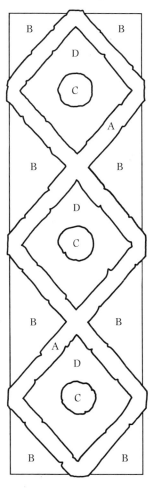

A formal herb border.

A Cotton lavender.
B Lady's mantle.
C Standard pyracantha.
D Catmint.

In different situations, and against different backgrounds box, germander, lavender or rue might be used for the hedging, whilst substituting pinks, thymes, dwarf white lavender or bronze bugle for the lady's mantle. In the centre the catmint could be replaced by purple sage, lavender 'Hidcote' or rosemary. Other plants which would make good standards in the centres of the diamonds are bay, holly, roses, privet or silver-leaved willows.

All these plants offer an infinite variety of shape, size and texture for both light and dark situations. When selecting the herb for the edging always choose a plant which contrasts with the infilling herbs.

A Small Suburban Herb Garden

A small garden filled with herbs is a practical and far more interesting alternative to the standard rectangular lawn enclosed on three sides with narrow flower borders. The design shown on page 21 may without too much difficulty be adapted to almost any small back garden. In this particular example the garden is roughly 40ft (12m) square, but the plan could easily be adapted to fit a larger or smaller area, or a rectangle. A number of existing trees and plants have been retained and incorporated into the new design – always bear in mind any existing worthwhile garden features or viewpoints.

The patio faces south and runs straight into a gravel 'lawn', which has been laid on a special black, woven groundsheet. This sheet is very effective in keeping the weeds down and is economical to lay. The gravel is soft and bright, reflecting useful light onto the surrounding tree trunks and dark, high fencing. In the four positions shown on the plan, broken paving stones have been positioned in a random pattern on blobs of mortar. The idea is that these areas should break up the sea of gravel and, at the same time, act as islands for low-growing herbs to nestle up against. The gravel can be kept off the flower beds by building a small retaining wall about two bricks high. A 2 × 4in (5 × 10cm) wooden edging, pre-treated with preservative, will work just as well, look just as attractive, and probably be more economical.

The advantages of this garden are two-fold. First, there are no hard textural differences between the various surfaces, so the eye is led gently from the patio to the far corner, giving a hint of more to come. Secondly, the garden needs no regular maintenance – two serious tidy-ups a year should ensure that it is kept under control.

A Large Herb Garden

When space allows, it is great fun to build a larger herb garden – the example shown on page 22 is some 50 × 60ft (15 × 18m) – with paths wide enough to take wheelchairs or baby carriages. With an area as large as this the planner can include a number of smaller theme gardens within the overall framework. These sub-gardens are an important feature of the design and add much to the visual effect and enjoyment of the garden. It is also worth noting that a garden of this scale can be planted with a range of herbs and scented plants so wide that they will ensure a satisfying garden from the early spring to late autumn. The box hedge around the centre circle is surrounded by four beds each with a colour theme. Great play is made throughout the garden of using short runs of low-growing herbs. In some places the plants will be clipped into a semi-formal shape (curry plant, winter savory, and cotton lavender); in other areas they will be left to strike a soft visual line along the bed (pinks and lady's mantle giving colour and scent). The thyme bed is planted with twelve different kinds of upright and creeping thymes. The small chamomile lawn is not too large and could be kept in condition quite easily. The rose beds are planted with a variety of old-fashioned roses, easily maintained and wafting plenty of sweet scent in midsummer. The garden also includes a silver border, a culinary bed, and a 'lawn' of woodruff, planted with spring-flowering bulbs, violets, and cowslips. The basic layout is simple and inexpensive to set up. Each bed is edged with treated wooden poles, cut to size, laid on the ground, and pegged in position. The paths are made up of a hardcore base and covered with gravel. The garden is designed to be walked through and is big enough to accommodate a number of seats at various points. Although not strictly formal in layout, this garden creates a sense of mystery with its simple, maze-like corridors that lead to delightful small herb gardens within the large garden.

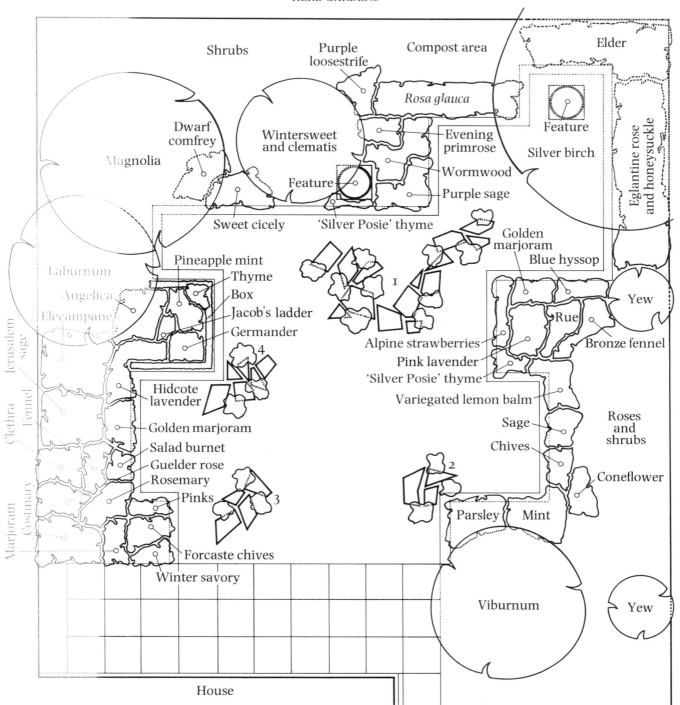

A herb-filled small garden.

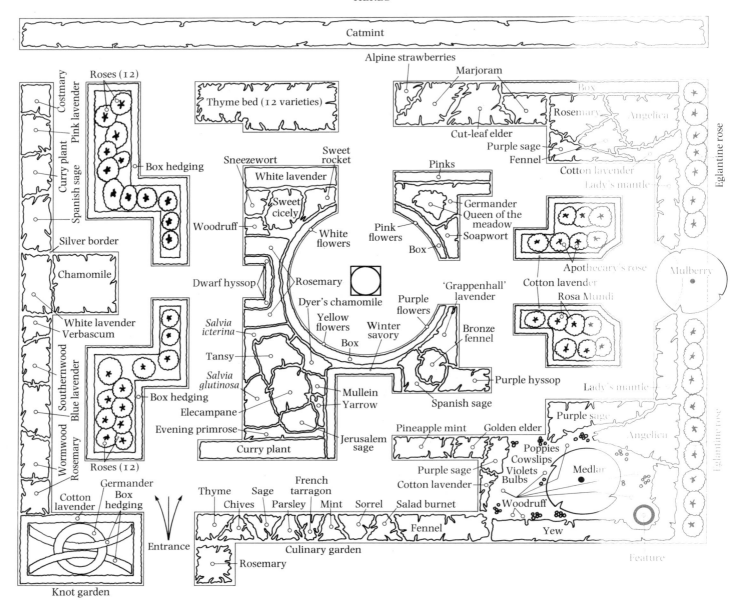

A large herb garden made up of a number of varied sub-gardens.

A Passageway Herb Garden

Passageways, patios, and paths are perfect areas for low-growing, creeping herbs. In fact, it is the crevices and cracks between the paving stones or bricks that create perfect places to plant chamomile and thymes. Two mints, pennyroyal and Corsican mint, are also worth considering. Pennyroyal, which has a large, bright green leaf, will spread quickly along a crack throughout the summer; the little

Corsican mint has a tiny, green leaf with an even smaller flower, which makes it perfect in minute cracks. Both tend to disappear in the winter, but will usually seed themselves and reappear if left undisturbed. Rupturewort, *Herniaria glabra*, is well worth considering where hard edges need to be broken visually and planting space is limited. A bright green, flat-growing, loose-knit plant, it grows quickly from a tiny crack to form a large, evergreen

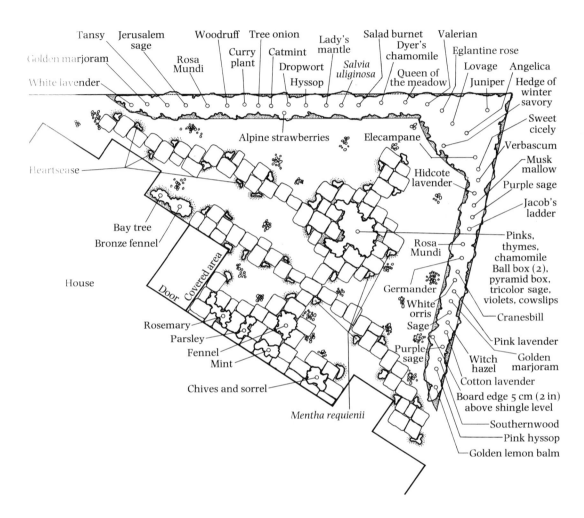

Tansy • Jerusalem sage • Golden marjoram • White lavender • Rosa Mundi • Woodruff • Curry plant • Tree onion • Catmint • Dropwort • Hyssop • Lady's mantle • Salvia uliginosa • Salad burnet • Dyer's chamomile • Queen of the meadow • Valerian • Eglantine rose • Lovage • Juniper • Angelica • Hedge of winter savory

Alpine strawberries • Elecampane • Sweet cicely • Verbascum • Musk mallow • Hidcote lavender • Purple sage • Jacob's ladder

Heartsease • Bay tree • Bronze fennel • House • Rosa Mundi • Pinks, thymes, chamomile • Ball box (2), pyramid box, tricolor sage, violets, cowslips

Door • Covered area • Germander • White orris • Sage • Cranesbill • Pink lavender

Rosemary • Parsley • Fennel • Mint • Purple sage • Witch hazel • Golden marjoram • Cotton lavender

Chives and sorrel • Board edge 5 cm (2 in) above shingle level

Mentha requienii • Southernwood • Pink hyssop • Golden lemon balm

A passageway herb garden.

mat that is easily controlled with a pair of pruning shears.

A logical place to grow culinary herbs is outside the kitchen door. This area might be merely a passageway alongside a house. The shape will often be irregular, which may be an advantage when it comes to designing an unusual and interesting, but above all usable, herb garden. The design shown is incorporated in a triangular-shaped area with each side about 20 ft (6 m) long extending away from the side of the house. Although it faces south it is overshadowed by the tall boundary fence, so it is important to create a feeling of light and space to offset any sense of being boxed in. Once again, gravel has been used as the primary surface; always good value, it is bright in colour and reflects the light well, it is relatively inexpensive to buy, it is easy to lay and it makes an excellent foil for the large herbs.

For practical reasons it has been necessary to create a 'carpet' herb garden so that it is possible to use the space without having the feeling of being hemmed in. The paving blocks are laid in an economical and informal way, but they do serve to create connecting pathways between the three exit points as well as making pockets for the culinaries outside the back door. The island in the centre of the garden is designed to give a little relief to the flatness around it; it is planted with upright thymes, flowering chamomile, and scented pinks. Three pieces of box topiary are included to give a little extra height in the middle of the bed. The narrow border around the edge is planted with herbs and aromatics, which act as a backcloth against the fence.

Herb Lawns

Herb lawns, usually of chamomile or thyme, are often considered to be low-maintenance alternatives to grass lawns, but they are extremely difficult to keep looking good. Chamomile and thyme are less tough than grass and they both seem to leave bald patches where their roots have not taken hold. A grass lawn is also easier to repair when worn.

A herb lawn will not bear very heavy traffic, so it is not to be advised where children constantly play or in any much-trodden part of the garden. Herb paths are tempting. The English philosopher Francis Bacon, in his essay 'Of Gardens' in 1625, advised setting 'whole Allies' of scented plants, 'to have the Pleasure, when you walk to tread', but his enthusiasm needs to be tempered with some practical caution. That said, there are few things more attractive on a summer day than strolling around the garden while one's lazy feet draw the scent from a herb lawn.

The herb lawn need not cover a vast area. Quite small plots may be planted at suitable points in the garden – rather like rugs in a room. Or a border of herbs may make a wide frame around a grass lawn. A mixed lawn is another possibility: herbs and grass may be interplanted – mints, for example, will grow companionably with grass provided that the lawnmower blades are not set too low.

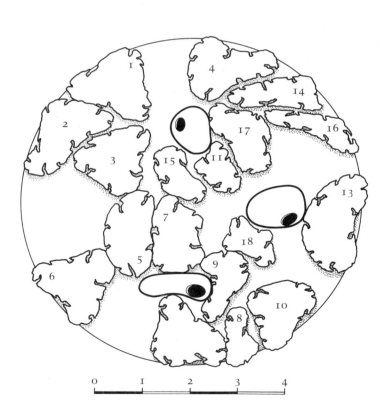

A thyme circle.

1 'E. B. Anderson'.
2 *T. albus*. 3 'Silver Posie'.
4 *T. coccineus*. 5 broad-leaf thyme. 6 gold thyme.
7 *T. mastochinus*.
8 *T. nitidus*. 9 lemon thyme. 10 *T. lanuginosus*.
11 'Wild Lemon'. 12 *Herba barona*. 13 'Doone Valley'.
14 'Annie Hall'. 15 'Golden Lemon'. 16 'Pink Chintz'.
17 'Porlock'. 18 *T. minimus*.

Chamomile

There are a number of different varieties, with different growing habits, of chamomile. There are single-flowered, double-flowered, and non-flowering varieties; all have scented leaves. The vigorous non-flowering variety *Anthemis nobilis* 'Treneague' is the best plant to use for a lawn. It is advisable to keep the chamomile area to a manageable size — 10 × 10ft (3 × 3m) square being about the maximum. The area to be planted must be well prepared, the site should be free-draining and free of all weeds and surface chips and stones, and it is a good idea to dig in some well-rotted manure prior to planting. Chamomiles should be planted in late spring, 6in (15cm) apart in each direction. The bed should be firmed with a light roller a couple of times during the summer to keep the plants flat and encourage the roots to take hold.

Thyme

Thymes, mass-planted, have a quite different appearance from chamomiles. In the first place they have flowers ranging in colour from white through to dark pink, and secondly there are quite a number of creeping varieties, all of which have different leaf colours, scents, and habits.

An unusual but appealing way to grow thymes is on their own, creating a patchwork of different varieties to give a most attractive massed effect. This could be either in a raised bed or at ground level and is a great idea for a sunny spot. The area shown on page 24 is a thyme circle at ground level, 6ft 6in (2m) in diameter, which is beautifully edged with Victorian roped edging tiles. The first task is to rake the earth level, removing all large surface stones. A thin sheet of black polythene should then be laid over the whole area and the thymes set in their positions. Cut a hole in the polythene around the root ball and plant the thyme through the polythene, gently firming down the soil around the plant. Clear off any excess soil from the polythene and cover it with a thin layer of grit. This will help conserve moisture and keep the weeds down. The thymes will spread happily over the grit and benefit from the reflected warmth. A few carefully chosen rocks or large stones should then be placed as required between some of the thymes. Such a thyme garden will be trouble-free and relatively weed-free; it will need very little maintenance — a simple trim of the spent flower stalks after flowering is all that will be required.

A Culinary Herb Corner

The design shown on page 26 is an effective way of creating a culinary herb corner within an existing garden. Because it is important that corner should be bright and cheerful, ornamental varieties of the popular culinaries have been used — golden marjoram, bronze fennel, 'Doone Valley' thyme, and purple sage. The bed is between 6ft (1.75m) and 10ft (3m) wide, which would be far too deep to reach the herbs at the back. This problem has been overcome by placing eight circular paving stones in the garden and extending the theme into the lawn.

Do not let the corner herb garden be too rigidly defined — the herbs should be allowed, or rather encouraged, to drift into and intermingle with the existing plants in the flower border; there should be no segregation here.

A Knot Garden

A knot garden is probably the most difficult garden to design; it also requires precision planting and a great deal of patience. The easiest way is to copy an existing garden or use a suitable illustration from a book. But if you want to design your own knot you must first draw it out on paper. You need to decide on a scale and to represent the hedges by two parallel lines about 9in (22.5cm) apart on the same scale. This will make it easier when it comes to sorting out which hedge is crossing which and which goes under and which goes over. Start by drawing a square and then fill in with a number of circles and lines, each crossing or striking each other and creating a regular pattern; then, taking one quarter at a time, decide which lines should make a continuous hedge, mark the plan accordingly, and repeat on the other three quarters.

The proposed site should be measured out accurately and marked with pegs and string along the straight lines. Curves and circles can be inscribed by using a stick on a length of string attached to a static pole as a compass; holding the string taut, draw the stick over the soil to mark the pattern. It can be a help to re-emphasize all the lines with a light-

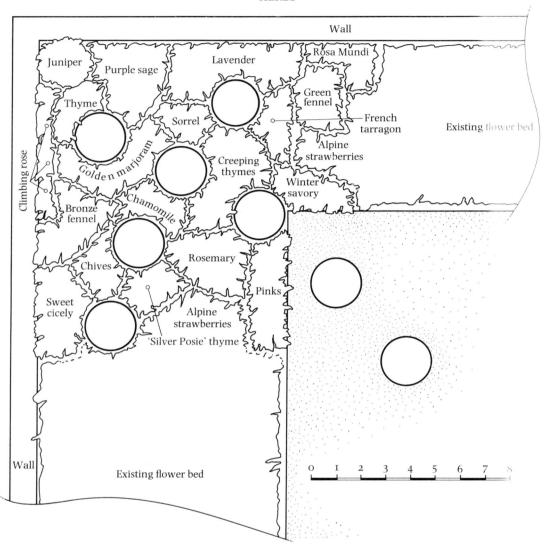

A garden corner filled with herbs for the kitchen.

coloured sand sprinkled along the ground. It is sensible to tackle a section at a time, re-marking damaged lines as necessary.

Planting the knot requires a careful choice of plant varieties – it is pointless to plant two very similar herbs together if what you are aiming at is a dramatic overall contrasting effect. Most of the herbs suitable for a knot garden – for example, green santolina, germander, dwarf hyssop, and box – should be planted between 9in (22.5cm) and 12in (30cm) apart. Dwarf box, however, should not be more than 4in (10cm) apart. If these planting distances are

observed it should be possible to achieve a neat, tight knot. While the hedges are growing it is most important not to be fooled by linear height. In order to encourage bottom growth the growing tips should be pinched out regularly during the first year – a heartbreaking job but quite essential. Once the knot is established, which will take between three and four years, the hedging should be clipped regularly, remembering that where different hedges cross and form the knot, the hedge that is supposedly going under should have its top curved down to a point where it meets the crossing hedge. This, of course,

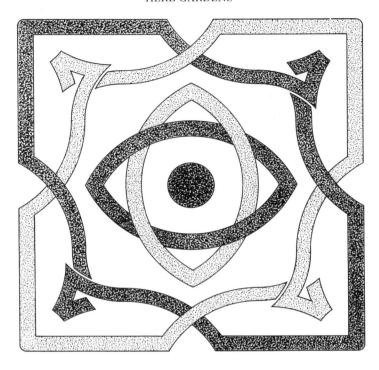

A traditional plan for a knot garden.

must be done on both sides of the crossing point. The top should then be curved back up to the correct level and continued at that level until the next sweep under.

Container Herbs

Containers in the form of urns, decorated flower pots, old chimney pots, and terracotta jars are all used extensively as features in herb gardens to add structure and interest. For those with no garden, containers become much more important as they may provide the only means of growing plants. Anything from an old tin bucket, basic flower pots, a pseudo-Roman urn, or a genuine Georgian window-box may be used to grow plants. Stone and terracotta tend to be the most sympathetic materials in the herb garden – not only are they natural colours and often of classical shapes, but they are also porous, helping to provide the best growing environment for plants that need good drainage.

A window-box is the most likely form of container for those with no garden – it can sit just as happily outside the kitchen door of a basement flat as it can on the windowsill of the 27th floor. Usually only 2ft (60cm) or, at most, 3ft (90cm) long, a window-box will have only enough space to grow a few herbs. In general, it is more satisfactory to try to mix culinary requirements with ornamental forms – purple sage, golden marjoram, silver thyme, and so on – which are all just as good as their green counterparts. Eight herbs is about the maximum possible in a window-box of average size and the most suitable are the smaller-growing herbs. Ideal perennial herbs for a window-box are: chives, parsley, thyme, winter savory, sweet marjoram, sorrel, and French tarragon. Most annual herbs will grow very well in a window-box. Sage and rosemary are quite possible for a short time, but will probably need replacing after a couple of years as they will grow too large in comparison with others. A single variety of herb can be very effective – all parsley would give plenty to pick as well as looking attractive.

None of the taller-growing, herbaceous perennials is suitable for growing in small containers –

A window-box of culinary herbs.

they will either grow far too large or need too much root space. Typically unsuitable herbs are fennel and lovage.

Urns and pots around the garden are much easier to fill, as there is an enormous variety of herbs that grow satisfactorily in containers. A half barrel with three types of mint – eau-de-Cologne, ginger mint, and pineapple mint – planted together and allowed to mix is very impressive and smells delicious. A terracotta pot, with pockets in the side, is a classic way to grow culinary herbs. A very satisfactory alternative, however, is to fill the whole pot with different varieties of thyme. When buying this kind of pot be sure to select a design that does not have too many pockets, ten being an absolute maximum for the largest pot; more than this and the plants will not have enough root space or food to allow them to grow successfully. Food and water are vital to any plants growing in a container – most composts have no more than six weeks' food available, so a regular feeding programme will be required. Use a liquid fertilizer every week throughout the growing season and always water into a saucer placed underneath the pot – this is the only way to ensure that all parts of the pot get equal amounts of moisture. There are really no satisfactory ways of keeping plants going for more than a year in a small container and it is courting disappointment to try. Herb pots and window-boxes should be stripped out and replanted with fresh compost each spring.

One of the reasons for growing your own culinary herbs is to ensure a fresh and plentiful supply of home-grown herbs to accompany your home-grown

vegetables – mint with new potatoes and peas, basil with tomatoes, savory with broad beans, sorrel with lettuce, and parsley with everything. A sensible and easy way to grow large quantities of fresh herbs is in a growing bag – here you will find all the necessary nutrients to ensure a good start to your herb crop, although it will, of course, need feeding after six weeks or so. The only remotely satisfactory way to grow herbs in the house is to set up a rotation system. Grow, say, a parsley, a chive, and a mint in pots on the kitchen windowsill and keep a duplicate set of pots, containing the same herbs, outside. After a week or so, bring the outside pots indoors, and try to keep up a succession in this way. Herbs make very bad house-plants, and are always best kept outside whenever possible.

Many of the great culinary herbs are annuals, with only one year's life, and are of little garden merit. Because of their short life and the need to produce plenty of foliage they make ideal subjects for growing in containers, where they will flourish if grown with the correct care – given a good compost (a mixture of peat and soil-based compost is ideal) and fed and watered regularly.

This almost seems to suggest that herbs in pots in the garden are of practical utility only and should be relegated to a hidden corner like the compost heap. But container-grown herbs can, of course, be used very positively to enhance the beauty of the garden. There is scope for creativity and ingenuity in arranging imaginative groupings of pots containing lush-foliaged or bright-flowered herbs to give life and colour to a perhaps not-too-successful part of

Herbs for cooking growing in a small herb pot.

the garden. Larger containers, including sinks, can be used singly for attractive arrangements of herbs following the same rules as have been suggested for the open ground. The choice of herbs is wide, though, when selecting larger herbs, avoid those that send down long tap roots, such as fennel and lovage; they will not be happy in the comparatively shallow soil of a container. Usually it is best to plant a tall herb or herbs in the middle of the container, arrange low-growing herbs all around, and use trailing herbs as edgings to droop over the sides of the pot and hide the line of its rim. If the pot is to have a permanent site, perhaps against a wall or in a corner, it may be more suitable to position large herbs at the back of their container.

A particular advantage of growing herbs in containers is that a pot may be moved around to fill temporary gaps between plants or holes left by gardening failures. If this is your intention, though, make sure the pot is not too heavy to carry. Fibreglass or plastic pots and containers are lighter and easier to move than those made of terracotta or stone; and soil-less composts lighter than those that are based on loam.

3

HERB GARDEN MAINTENANCE

Herbs are known for two distinctive properties – one is a tendency for the long, fleshy stems of the herbaceous varieties to fall over during wet and windy weather, the other is their habit of proliferating at an alarming rate, either by root-running or self-seeding. With some careful planning both these problems can be overcome without too much hard work. The solution to the first problem is simple – once the herb border is planted and the herbs established, insert some retaining hoops around the taller-growing plants. The late spring is an ideal time to do this. Although not pretty to look at until the plant has grown through the hoop, it is much easier to position correctly beforehand and, at the speed most herbs grow, it will not take very long before the hoop is hidden.

The invasive herbs are more of a problem because you do not always want to build a fortress around the mints! The simplest ways to stop a herb running are: first, to plant it in a container; second, to surround it with bricks or paving stones; and third, to bury a slate or plastic surround around the area within which you wish to contain the roots. (This is not fool-proof, but it will help a great deal and is ideally suited when a plant has to be contained in an informal situation such as an herbaceous border.) If you do not need to make your own shape, you can quite easily use the top 6in (15cm) of a flower pot, or a bucket with the bottom knocked out. Plant the herb in the middle and set the container in the ground with the top edge just above the soil.

The sensible way to avoid random self-seeding is to cut off the dead flower-heads before the seeds are ripe and falling. With many herbs this option is an easy decision – orach, lovage, angelica, and burdock are all better for being trimmed before the plant begins to die back; however, others that retain an interesting structural form, such as teasel and fennel, are best left, in which case they will scatter their seed. This should be hoed out; otherwise it will germinate in the spring.

Most herb gardens require two major maintenance sessions a year – one in the autumn, the other in late spring. Throughout the growing season, weeds and unwanted seedlings should be hoed out regularly. Some low-growing varieties of herbs, for example marjorams, sometimes collapse after heavy summer storms and their centres open out. They can be cut back at that time without harm and will regrow very quickly.

Autumn
Autumn is the season when plants have died down and flowering species have given of their best. During this time, cut back lavender plants gently to tidy them and trim off all dead flower heads; similarly, cut off dead rose flowers unless their hips are of special merit. As herbaceous plants die down, cut back to ground level. If any major replanting is planned it is a good idea to place a stake or bamboo to mark where plants are before they vanish underground for the winter. When the deciduous trees, such as elders, have shed their leaves in late autumn they can be pruned to keep their shape under control. Elders can be cut back to within 2ft (60cm) of the ground without coming to harm. Most of the

other herbs should be left well alone at this time of year. Tidy up, but do not cut back too hard – this should be left until the spring.

Spring

It is never easy to decide when spring has begun. However, it is vital not to be fooled by the lure of a false dawn – if you are tempted to begin pruning too early on a warm, sunny, late-winter day you may well regret it later when frost gets into the young growth and causes damage. It is best to wait until the plants show signs of strong, new growth and the chances of heavy frosts have receded before starting hard pruning and cutting-back. Herbs such as lavenders, savories, cotton lavenders, rue, hyssop, and southernwood should now be cut back down to the lowest signs of young growth, to give the plants or hedges a neat, tidy shape. The Mediterranean woody herbs – rosemary, sage, and thyme – resent being cut back hard at any time and are best just gently trimmed, or even pinched out between finger and thumb throughout the growing season. On no account should you cut back into the old wood.

Herbs are generally considered uncomplicated plants that grow happily in poor soils, but, in our experience, herbs in the garden do better if mulched with well-rotted manure every two years in the spring – this will give the plants some food and help them retain moisture through any periods of drought in the summer, as well as giving their roots some protection through the bad winters.

Culinary herbs will be weakened by continual cutting throughout the year; in time this may discourage the plant from growing at all. Two ways to avoid this are:

1 Grow enough plants of any particular variety to allow for regrowth before further cutting. All the annuals can easily and cheaply be produced from seed, and should always be grown in quantity, with new seed planted as required.

2 Feed the plants regularly throughout the growing season either with a liquid feed in the watering system or a dressing of fertilizer raked into the soil.

Herb hedges are usually made up of several varieties of evergreen herbs with quite different growing habits. Box needs an initial trim once the new growth is distorting the shape, with a further trim in June to keep the sides and top square. Santolinas, germanders, and most other hedging herbs grow faster than box and therefore should be cut back hard each spring and trimmed regularly throughout the summer to keep their shape and stop them flowering.

Propagation is generally dealt with in the descriptions of the individual herbs. However, it might be helpful to give general guidance on growing annuals from seed. As commercially bought seed always has plenty in a packet, sow a few seeds little and often throughout the summer – this will allow enough plants for cropping and for providing a surplus to preserve for winter use. It is best to start with fresh seed every year rather than keep old seed from year to year.

Fill a seed tray with a proprietary seed compost and firm it down. Sprinkle a little seed thinly and evenly over the compost. Label the tray and water with a fine spray. Cover the seed tray with a piece of plastic, preferably black, and put it into a warm place for the seeds to germinate – an airing cupboard is perfect. Check every day, and as soon as the seeds show signs of shoots, remove the tray from the dark and place it on a light shelf or windowsill, making sure that the shoots do not burn in bright sunlight. Once the seedlings are about $\frac{1}{2}$in (1cm) tall and have their first pair of true leaves, it is time to prick them out into individual flower pots. Using a $3\frac{1}{2}$in (9cm) pot, carefully separate the seedlings and replant them, three to a pot, in a standard potting mix. Water well and leave to grow on in a warm, light place. When the plants have made good growth, and are about 3in (7.5cm) high, with their roots showing through the base of the pots, it is time to plant into the garden. Choose a spring day when no risk of frost remains and plant the young herbs into the border. Pinch out the growing tips, continue to water well, and allow the herb plants to grow on for a few weeks before cropping.

A culinary herb garden
A generous assortment of culinary herbs growing in a formal garden divided into triangular beds by brick and stone paths; a sundial gives a focus of interest.

A scented border
Growing happily together (above) are white goat's rue (*Galega officinalis* 'Alba'), *Salvia verticillata*, catmint (*Nepeta mussinii*), and curry plant (*Helichrysum angustifolium*).

A knot garden
This small knot garden (top), although only one year old, already shows the different growth rates of the box (*Buxus sempervirens*) used for the outer edge and central square, the germander (*Teucrium chamaedrys*) that forms the circle, and the cotton lavender (*Santolina chamaecyparissus*) that makes the semicircles. All the hedges were clipped well back when young to encourage low bushy growth.

Herbs in pots
An attractive group of herb pots (left) of various styles, shapes, and sizes planted with, left to right, alpine strawberries, scented geraniums, mixed thymes, and an assortment of herbs and, front centre, parsley.

35

Angelica
An imposing plant, angelica
(*Angelica archangelica*) (left)
may reach a height of 10ft (3m)
and needs plenty of space if it is
to show at its best. Seen against
the sky, the full glory of its
strong but delicate structure is
revealed.

Variegated lemon balm
Refreshingly lemon scented, as its popular name proclaims, variegated lemon balm (*Melissa officinalis* 'Variegata') (above), with its green leaves splashed with pale gold, is attractive all summer long.

Lady's mantle
A mass of pale green, downy foliage and soft yellow flowers, lady's mantle (*Alchemilla vulgaris*) (left) comes into its own after a shower of rain, when the leaves are covered in tiny drops of silver.

Bay
The bay (*Laurus nobilis*) (left), the 'noble laurel' of the ancient Romans, merits its place in the herb garden on both culinary and decorative grounds. One of its qualities is that it may be trained in a variety of topiary shapes – ball, pyramid, or column.

Bergamot
Monarda didyma 'Cambridge Scarlet' (right) is the most beautiful and the most fragrant of the bergamots; it is a joy in the herb garden when in full flower in late summer.

Box
A decorated urn nestles against a small, clipped hedge of variegated box (*Buxus sempervirens* 'Elegantissima') (left). The bright edges of the leaves will lighten any dark corner and the dense habit makes it an ideal hedge plant for a knot garden.

Borage
The pointed, hairy leaves and mauve-blue flowers – in legend the colour of the Virgin Mary's robes – of borage (*Borago officinalis*) (opposite, top left) make it a desirable resident of the garden. Accommodatingly, it is not hard to propagate.

Camphor
The silver-green leaves of camphor (*Balsamita vulgaris* 'Tomentosum') (opposite, top right) and its white flowers, when they emerge, mix happily with the silvers and pinks of other herbs in the garden.

Catmint
A wide border of catmint (*Nepeta mussinii*) (opposite, bottom left) almost overwhelms a garden seat. The lightly fragrant spikes of lavender-blue flowers, which last throughout the summer, attract bees and butterflies.

Double-flowered chamomile
'The more it is trodden, the more it will spread' promises an old proverb of the chamomile. The double-flowered form (*Anthemis nobilis flore pleno*) (opposite, bottom right) covers the ground with mats of apple-scented foliage, topped with cream-coloured flowers.

Curry plant and horsemint

Two herbs with silver-green foliage – curry plant (*Helichrysum angustifolium*) and horsemint (*Mentha longifolia*) – make a colour-coordinated group in a border (right), culminating in late summer in a haze of yellow and purple flowers that will attract bees and butterflies from all around.

Chives

Used either in a single clump or en masse as an edging, chives (*Allium schoenoprasum*) (top left), with their round purple flower heads, make a colourful addition to the border. If dead flower heads are removed there will be a second showing later in the year.

Dwarf comfrey

Dwarf comfrey (*Symphytum grandiflorum*) (centre left) is a useful plant for difficult or shady areas. The dark green foliage spreads readily and the creamy, drooping flowers last for several months.

Cowslip

A pretty, delicately scented herb, flowering in the early spring, the cowslip (*Primula veris*) (bottom left) brightens a sunny corner of the herb garden with its yellow-gold petals.

Purple elder

With its dark bronze foliage and cream flowers splashed with pink, the purple elder (*Sambucus nigra* 'Purpurea') (left) is a fragrant shrub that magnificently provides height and colour to the back of a herb border.

Elecampane

The elecampane (*Inula helenium*) (right), with its enormous leaves, dandelion-yellow flowers, and its towering height – it easily reaches 7ft (2m) – is the monarch of the herb garden.

Foxglove

The tapering spires of purple or white flowers of the common foxglove (*Digitalis purpurea*) (right) look splendid when the herb is used for under-planting in a bed of old roses. The foxglove also looks fittingly at home in a wild garden.

Cranesbill
The strongly aromatic leaves of the cranesbill (*Geranium macrorrhizum*) (above left) turn a beautiful colour in the autumn; the pretty pink flowers appear in late spring.

Germander
The germander (*Teucrium chamaedrys*) (above) is a small evergreen shrub that can be clipped to form a neat, dark, evergreen hedge; it bears pink flowers in early summer.

American honeysuckle
The dark pink buds of the American honeysuckle (*Lonicera × americana*) (left) open to pink and yellow florets that fade to cream as they age. This vigorous, fragrant, twining climber flowers through the summer.

Queen of the meadow
An imposing herb that grows up to 8ft (2.4m) tall, queen of the meadow (*Eupatorium purpureum*) (right) bears flower heads in shades of pink that seem to be covered with bees and butterflies on warm, sunny, summer days.

Pink hyssop
All the hyssops are valuable for
hedging, for knot gardens, and
for planting in borders, but the
pink-flowered form (*Hyssopus
officinalis* 'Roseus') (right) is the
most decorative and perhaps the
most unusual to find in a herb
garden.

Anise hyssop
The bright purple flowers of the
mint-like anise hyssop
(*Agastache anethiodora*) (far
right) are an irresistible
attraction to bees. The aniseed-
scented foliage makes, for
humans, a delicious tea.

Golden hop
A useful and attractive herbaceous climber, the vigorous, fast-growing golden hop (*Humulus lupulus* 'Aureus') (left) quickly covers a wall, fence, or pergola with its bright vine-shaped leaves.

Orris root
One of the irises grown for the commercial production of orris root is *Iris pallida* (right), which in the herb garden is valued for its shapely, sword-shaped foliage, which adds a neat, unfussy shape to a border.

Cotton lavender and lady's mantle
Cotton lavender (*Santolina chamaecyparissus*) and lady's mantle (*Alchemilla vulgaris*) are two versatile plants (above) that combine well not only with one another but with many other plants.

Lavenders

The old English lavenders, with their various flower colours, mix well when grown together, although they still retain their separate identities. Here the dark 'Hidcote' stands, distinct but neighbourly, alongside the soft 'Loddon Pink'. As they have similar habits, they can be clipped and pruned as one.

White musk mallow
This musk mallow (*Malva moschata* 'Alba') (right) is one of the most beautiful of garden herbs when it is in pink-centred flower and the delicate, translucent white petals are massed among the finely cut, bright green leaves.

Purple loosestrife
The purple loosestrife (*Lythrum salicaria*) (left), which grows to 8ft (2.4m) tall, produces striking flower-covered bayonets of rich colour late in the season.

Lovage
Lovage (*Levisticum officinale*) (left) grows to at least 6ft (1.8m) and makes an impressive and handsome plant, with its glossy green leaves and, in early summer, its clusters of tiny yellow flowers.

Pot marigold
The small pot marigold
(*Calendula officinalis*), with its
cheerful orange flowers, stands
out (above) against a
background provided by the
lace-like foliage of a young
bronze fennel (*Foeniculum
vulgare* 'Purpureum').

Compact marjoram
The fragrant leaves of the
compact marjoram (*Origanum
vulgare* 'Compactum') (right)
make a thick, fragrant cushion
of bright green that will be
covered with pink flowers in the
summer months.

Golden marjoram, southernwood, and catmint
Golden marjoram (*Origanum vulgare* 'Aureum'), here (left) with the sun making its leaves aglow, mingles harmoniously in a blend of soft, muted colors with southernwood (*Artemisia abrotanum*) and catmint (*Nepeta mussinii*).

Pineapple mint and rue
The pineapple mint (*Mentha rotundifolia* 'Variegata') is the finest garden form of mint, although it is the least interesting in the kitchen. Here (right) its irregularly variegated foliage in shades from white to silver-green contrasts with the steel blue of a rue (*Ruta graveolens* 'Jackman's Blue').

Red orach
The translucent foliage of the red orach (*Atriplex hortensis* 'Rubra') contrasts here (right) with the purple-veined leaves of the bloody dock (*Rumex sanguineus*) and the red flowers of a valerian (*Centranthus ruber*). Tiny flowers of self-seeded heartsease peep through the surrounding foliage.

Garden mint
The most popular of the mints for food flavouring, mint (*Mentha spicata*) (above left) is a fragrant and decorative garden plant, producing attractive mauve flowers by the end of summer.

Parsley
One of the commonest and most easily recognizable of the culinary herbs, parsley (*Petroselinum crispum*) (left) is underrated as a garden plant. With its uniquely crinkled, bright green leaves it makes an attractive low-growing border plant.

Cheddar pink
Of the many herbs that make excellent subjects for wall pots, the Cheddar pink (*Dianthus caesius*) (left) is perhaps the most useful and successful; the silvery leaves survive all year and the scented flowers last all summer.

Poppy 'Ladybird'
With its scarlet, black-blotched petals, this poppy (*Papaver commutatum* 'Ladybird') (below) makes a stunning display when mass planted; if the flowers are removed as they die, it will bloom all summer long.

Evening primrose
The cup-shaped flowers of the evening primrose (*Oenothera biennis*) (above) open at dusk throughout the summer, the fragile petals glowing in the last of the day's sunshine.

Sweet rocket
The sweet rocket (*Hesperis matronalis*) (right) is a true cottage-garden flower, grown for its medicinal qualities and for the beauty of its pale purple flowers in midsummer. It was known in England as the vesper flower because its scent is strongest in the evening.

Rosa Mundi
This showy old shrub rose (*Rosa gallica* 'Versicolor') (above), with semi-double flowers splashed and striped with pinks, has been known since before the 16th century. A good-natured plant, very floriferous, with abundant foliage, it can withstand hard pruning.

Eglantine rose
The leaves of the eglantine rose (*Rosa eglanteria*) (right) are sweetly scented – hence its other common name, sweet brier. Its single flowers are followed in autumn by bright red hips. Strong, sharp thorns make it an excellent rose for an informal, impenetrable hedge.

Rosemary
The hardy evergreen rosemary (*Rosmarinus officinalis*) (above), with its fragrant, needle-like leaves and small, pale blue flowers, is one of the foundation plants of any herb garden. It can be used as a hedging plant, being amenable to clipping and shaping, or planted in a border.

Purple sage
The beautiful reddish-purple leaves – sometimes splashed with cream – of the purple sage (*Salvia officinalis* 'Purpurea') (right) make a stunning cushion of colour in the herb garden. The sages are among the oldest-known of the healing herbs.

Sage
The downy, grey-green leaves of the garden sage (*Salvia officinalis*) (right) – the common culinary form – contrast with the sword-like leaves of the orris, or London flag (*Iris germanica*), planted in the background.

Salvias
Salvias (opposite, top) live companionably together in a border – the red-flowered pineapple sage (*Salvia rutilans*), *S. fulgens*, and the blue-flowered *S. patens* make a wonderful display of blossom that lasts for months.

Creeping savory
The small, spicily aromatic leaves of the creeping savory (*Satureja repandra*) carpet a rockery (opposite, bottom) and are bespattered with tiny white flowers in late summer.

Winter savory
Winter savory (*Satureja montana*) (far left) is an evergreen shrub that bears tiny pink flowers in late summer. The narrow, dark green leaves have a delicious spicy flavour and were once used as a household disinfectant, either strewn on floors or burned on fires.

Sorrel
The light green leaves – sometimes silver-blotched when young – of sorrel (*Rumex scutatus*) make here (left) a solid mass of foliage. These sharp-flavoured leaves may be eaten raw in salads, cooked as a vegetable like spinach, used to season soups and sauces, or infused to make sorrel tea.

Sweet cicely
The small, white florets of sweet cicely (*Myrrhis odorata*) (above) appear in early spring and provide bees with some of the earliest nectar of the year. The fern-like foliage makes a soft but majestic display. The fruits turn dark brown when ripe and, eaten raw, have a nutty flavour.

Teasel
The stately teasel (*Dipsacus fullonum*) (right) grows to 6ft (2m) tall and adds statuesque form to any garden. Its pale mauve, thistle-like flower heads are responsible for its old common name, fuller's thistle. It was traditionally used to 'tease', or raise the nap, of cloth.

73

Thyme

The garden thyme (*Thymus vulgaris*) (left) is perhaps the most highly flavoured and the most useful to the cook of all the thymes. It is also the most commonly cultivated – it makes an attractive green cushion of leaves, can be clipped to form a low-growing hedge, or used as an edging.

Thyme 'Doone Valley'

One of the several varieties of thyme useful to the herb gardener, the prostrate 'Doone Valley' (above) creeps over the soil to make a neat, ground-covering mat of lemon-scented, gold-variegated foliage. The small, clustered flowers are attractive to honey bees – and thyme honey is said to be best of all.

Valerian

An ancient healing herb, whose root in particular has medicinal value (and, according to legend, was used by the Pied Piper to lure away the rats of Hamelin). Valerian (*Valeriana officinalis*) (left), with its neat clusters of florets, is a valuable addition to the summer herb garden.

Lemon verbena

An ideal plant to grow in a tub on a patio, lemon verbena (*Aloysia triphylla*) (bottom left) is easily shaped for topiary work. The pointed, lemon-scented leaves dry well and retain their fragrance for a very long time; they are a near-indispensable ingredient of pot-pourris.

Heartsease

The heartsease (*Viola tricolor*), the parent of the cultivated pansy, self-seeds readily and its flowers (which are sometimes only bicoloured) add touches of colour throughout the garden. Here they make a striking contrast with the plain foliage of toadflax (*Linaria vulgaris*). An infusion made from the flowers is reputed to ease a lover's broken heart – hence the common name.

Violet

The sweetly scented violet (*Viola odorata*) (left) is one of the first flowers of spring. The flowers – whose colour has given an adjective to the English language – mix prettily with primroses and cowslips. The heart-shaped leaves make a soothing ointment. Violets should never be given to singers – folk legend has it that the scent paralyzes the vocal chords.

Dyer's chamomile and viper's bugloss
It is the toothed leaves of dyer's chamomile (*Anthemis tinctoria*) that are aromatic, but the golden daisy-like flowers that provided a yellow-brown dye are of more decorative value in the garden. They are set here (left) against the deep blue of viper's bugloss (*Echium vulgare*), which, like the chamomile, flowers throughout the summer.

Wintergreen

The shiny, leathery, evergreen leaves of wintergreen (*Gaultheria procumbens*) (right) form a low, close mat. The white, bell-shaped flowers show late in the year and are followed by large, fleshy, scarlet flowers that last until the spring. Wintergreen oil, whose main ingredient is a chemical related to aspirin, has been used since early times to soothe headaches.

Woodruff

In early summer the tiny white flowers of the woodruff (*Asperula odorata*) dapple the foliage in a shady corner of the garden. It is the shape of the shiny green leaves as they cluster around the stems that give the plant the 'ruff' part of its name. The whole plant is aromatic, but it is the leaves that give off, when they are dry, the familiar scent of new-mown hay that in the past made woodruff a popular strewing herb.

4

A SELECTION OF GARDEN HERBS

ANGELICA
Angelica archangelica (Umbelliferae)
Biennial or triennial.   see page 36

___

Origins   Native to north Europe and Asia.
Ultimate size   Up to 10 × 3 ft (3 × 1 m).
Soil   Angelica grows most happily on slightly damp ground, on river banks, or in meadows.
Sun/shade   Will grow largest and most spectacularly in part shade, but will happily tolerate full sun.
Description   A large, very stately plant with bright green leaves and young stems, which redden with age. The flower heads, which usually appear in the third year in May, can be up to 12 in (30 cm) in diameter, with pale green florets. It is sometimes possible to extend the life of the plant by another year by cutting off the flower spikes before they develop. Once the plant has flowered and set seed, in early July, it will die.
Position   A good plant for the back of a border, it looks good planted alongside fennels and queen of the meadow, which take over when the angelica has died down in July.
Propagation   If the seeds are allowed to ripen and drop in midsummer, an abundance of seedlings will appear for the following year. The surplus can, of course, simply be hoed out in the spring.
Use   The stems are often candied as a cake decoration (angelica should be cropped in the second or third year in early May, before the stems have hardened and become tough). It is also an important ingredient in some liqueurs.
Others   Wild angelica (*Angelica sylvestris*) is similar in appearance to cultivated angelica but is not usually used in cooking. The roots yield a yellow dye.

___

ANISE HYSSOP
Agastache anethiodora (Labiatae)
Perennial.   see page 48

___

Origins   South America.
Ultimate size   3 × 1 ft (90 × 30 cm).
Soil   Ordinary, well-drained.
Sun/shade   Grows best in full sun.
Description   The fairly large, softly purple leaves have a strong scent of aniseed. The plant produces beautiful spikes of bright purple flowers that last all summer and will dry well if cut in early August.
Position   A large clump of about six plants makes a very striking feature in the herb garden when in full bloom, planted in the centre of a bed, perhaps alongside a scarlet bergamot or white musk mallow. It is especially attractive to bees.
Propagation   Easily grown from seeds collected the previous year.
Use   The dried leaves are good in a pot-pourri.
Others   *Agastache foeniculum* and *A. mexicana* are very similar plants with dark blue or purple flowers.

___

BASIL
Ocimum basilicum (Labiatae)
Annual.

___

Origins   Native to India, grown in Mediterranean lands for thousands of years.

Ultimate size   12 × 6in (30 × 15cm).
Soil   Rich, very well-drained.
Sun/shade   Full sun.
Description   Large, fleshy, green leaves with a wonderfully aromatic scent when bruised.
Position   Very suitable as a pot-grown herb, it flourishes on a well-lit windowsill.
Propagation   Basil grows quickly and easily from seed, but it is vital not to sow too early – the tender young seedlings will damp off at the slightest hint of cold or wet.
Use   Basil is *the* herb to eat with home-grown tomatoes. Tear it into shreds and add it also to salads and fresh pasta sauces. The best way to preserve the flavour for the winter months is to soak plenty of leaves in a jar of bland cooking oil for several weeks, strain off, and seal in a clean jar.
Others   The dwarf bush basil (*Ocimum minimum*) has a very similar taste. Lettuce-leaf basil (*O. crispum*) has large crinkled leaves and there is also a lemon-scented basil (*O. citriodorum*).

BAY
Laurus nobilis (Lauraceae)
Shrub or small tree.   see page 38

Origins   Native to Europe and Asia Minor.
Ultimate size   Up to 15 ft (4.5 m).
Soil   Any well-drained soil. If grown in containers, bays should be fed with a liquid feed weekly during the growing season – April to September.
Sun/shade   Best in full sun, but will tolerate deep shade.
Description   Dark green, leathery leaves with a pronounced scent. Small, yellow flowers in spring. Although bays grow naturally into medium-sized trees, they are often grown in containers and clipped into shapes – pyramids, balls, or standards.
Position   Bay is native to Mediterranean countries and should, therefore, be grown in a position suited to its potentially fragile nature. When planted in the garden it is wise to site it in a spot well sheltered from the cold winter winds, which may not kill the plant but may badly burn the leaves. In cold districts it is wiser to grow bay in pots and bring these inside during the worst of the winter.

If a bay is to be grown permanently in a pot, treatment has to be more careful than if it were in the ground. In summer, water will be very important – bays can take being in a comparatively small pot for their size, but because of this will need watering more often – perhaps daily in high summer. Feeding will be vital for a pot-grown plant – a nitrogen food is the ideal way to encourage leaves for use in cooking – so feed weekly during the growing season. In winter, feeding should be stopped and pot-grown plants should be watered only when the soil looks very dry. However, care will have to be taken to protect the tree from the winter cold – the roots are far more vulnerable to cold damage when they are above ground. It would be sensible to bring the pot into a frost-free room if at all possible – a garage, garden-room, or summer house should suffice if an unheated greenhouse is not available.
Propagation   Bay is usually grown from cuttings taken in late summer; it is slow to root and needs bottom heat and patience.
Use   The leaves are used fresh or dried as a flavouring for soups, stews, sauces, and so on. It is sometimes used in liqueurs.

Others A particularly attractive form of bay tree is one with golden leaves – *Laurus nobilis* 'Aurea'. In spring the young foliage is a wonderful bright yellow. Another form is the willow-leaf bay (*L. n. angustifolia*), which has thin, narrow leaves and tends to grow slightly smaller. Both can be used in the same way as green bay.

BERGAMOT
Monarda didyma (Labiatae)
Perennial.   see page 38

Origins Native to North America, naturalized in South America.

Ultimate size 3 ft × 1 ft 6 in (90 × 45 cm).

Soil Grows best in rich, moist soil. A native to the American woods, bergamot appreciates cool roots. In cold soils bergamots tend to be short lived.

Sun/shade Partial shade with sun some of the day.

Description This is one of the most decorative plants for the herb garden, the bright crimson flowers at the tops of the stems coming in late summer, when much else has finished. The leaves have a wonderfully, sweet fragrance when crushed.

Position A good plant for the centre of a border or the edge of a 'wild' path, where the scented leaves can be touched.

Propagation Although bergamot can be grown from seed very easily, to guarantee the same flower colour it is necessary to take tip cuttings in the summer, before flowering, or to split the plant in the autumn, replanting the young, outer roots and discarding the dead centre of the plant.

Use The scented leaves make a pleasant drink, with a perfume similar to that of the bergamot-orange oil used in Earl Grey teas. The flowers make a very good ingredient in a pot-pourri. The oil is sometimes used in the cosmetic industry.

Others Bergamot can also be found with flowers in shades of pink, purple, red, and white. The wild bergamot (*Monarda fistulosa*) has purple flowers. Lemon bergamot (*M. citriodora*), is an annual with very spectacular heads of purple bracts in late summer. The leaves have a strong, lemon scent.

BORAGE
Borago officinalis (Boraginaceae)
Annual.   see page 40

Origins Native to the Mediterranean region.

Ultimate size 3 × 1 ft (90 × 30 cm).

Soil Loose, well-drained.

Sun/shade Full sun.

Description A very hairy plant, with soft down up the stems and over the leaves. Very pretty, blue flowers with black calyxes appear in profusion all summer and continue until cut down by the first heavy frosts.

Position Ideally grown toward the front of a border in a fairly large clump.

Propagation Borage self-seeds easily, so little work is needed to have new plants the next season. A few flowering plants left to die in the autumn will ensure that plenty of seed is scattered around to germinate early in the next spring. Bees find borage most attractive.

Use Borage flowers have little taste, but they add

instant magic when scattered on to a salad or added to a summer wine cup. The young leaves taste of cucumber and can be shredded in salads. Candied flowers are used in cake decoration.

Others There is a white form that, although unusual, does not have quite the same magic appeal. *Borago laxiflora* is a prostrate perennial with small, dark green, hairy leaves and the same stunning, deep blue flowers all summer.

BOX
Buxus sempervirens (Buxaceae)
Evergreen shrub or tree.   see pages 35 and 40

Origins Native to Europe and north Africa.
Ultimate size From 1 ft 6 in (45 cm) to 12 ft (3.5 m).
Soil Ordinary.
Sun/shade Either.
Description Not strictly a useful herb by today's definition, box is traditionally thought of as the perfect edging for the herb garden, be it a tiny hedge only 8 in (20 cm) high, or a larger hedge of about 2 ft (60 cm). Slow-growing and infinitely clippable, with small, dark green, aromatic, leathery leaves, box is perfect in most situations. Many herb gardens badly need extra structure during the dormant season when the larger plants have died down, and topiary box is, of course, perfect for this.
Propagation Nearly always grown from cuttings, box roots slowly, but readily, when taken with a heel of old wood and planted in sandy soil, in a shady spot.
Use Despite having originally been used medicin-

ally and for woodwork, the main use today is for making hedges and shaped, specimen plants. Box wood, which is very hard, is still used to make musical instruments and ornate boxes.
Others There are several varieties of box. The dwarf edging box, *Buxus sempervirens* 'Suffruticosa', grows to about 1 ft (30 cm); *B. sempervirens* 'Rotundifolia' has rounded leaves and is especially good for topiary work; *B. sempervirens* 'Aurea' has pretty golden leaves; and *B. sempervirens* 'Elegantissima' has variegated foliage.

CAMPHOR
Balsamita vulgaris 'Tomentosum' (Compositae)
Perennial.   see page 40

Origins Native to Asia Minor.
Ultimate size Up to 18 in (45 cm) in midsummer when in flower × 2 ft (60 cm).
Soil Any well-drained soil.
Sun/shade Full sun.
Description The silver-green leaves have a strong camphor scent when crushed, and pretty, white, daisy-like flowers are borne in late summer.
Position Camphor is a slightly difficult plant to position, as the leaves are at their best in early summer, when they are still very silver and close to the ground. It really has to be sited toward the back of a border as the flowering shoots are quite tall. It looks quite wonderful when planted alongside pink musk mallows.
Propagation The plant can be split into small sections in the autumn, and replanted as required in the garden.

Use When added to a pot-pourri the dried leaves help to deter moths.

Others A very similar plant is alecost or costmary (*Chrysanthemum balsamita*), which has silver leaves with a strong, minty smell. Unfortunately, the flowers, borne in late summer, are rather dreary and groundsel-like.

CATMINT
Nepeta mussinii (Labiatae)
Perennial.   see pages 35, 40 and 59

Origins A native to Iran.
Ultimate size To about 16 × 16 in (40 × 40 cm).
Soil Ordinary, well-drained.
Sun/shade Full sun.
Description The grey-blue leaves have a recognizable scent, often very attractive to cats. The blue flowers appear in mid-June and last most of the summer. Catmint needs planting in a sheltered spot in the garden, protected from the winter winds. It is a good idea to leave the dead branches on the plant all winter to help protect the young growth, which appears before the worst weather is really over, and then give the plant a good clean-up in the spring.
Position Catmint looks its best when grown alongside a path stretching into the distance. It is also a wonderful plant to grow among a bed of old-fashioned roses.
Propagation Best divided by splitting the roots during the autumn or spring.
Use The aromatic leaves have been used to add scent to pot-pourris, but are more often used commercially to add bulk when stuffing catnip mice for cats to play with.

Others Smaller-growing forms of catmint can be found, growing to about 8 in (20 cm), and there is a form with much darker flowers. Catnip (*Nepeta cataria*) is a less exciting plant, growing much taller, with dull, white flowers in late summer.

CHAMOMILE, DOUBLE-FLOWERED
Anthemis nobilis flore pleno (Compositae)
Perennial.   see page 40

Origins Europe.
Ultimate size 6 × 12 in (15 × 30 cm).
Soil Ordinary, well-drained.
Sun/shade Sun.
Description A ground-hugging chamomile with wonderfully scented leaves when crushed, it is usually grown for the pretty, double, button flowers.
Position Planted at spacings of about 3 in (7.5 cm), the plantlets will gradually spread laterally to make an attractive, sweetly scented lawn. The only disadvantage with using this chamomile rather than the non-flowering form is that it will need a gentle mow two or three times during the growing season. Perhaps the most satisfactory place to grow double chamomile is in the cracks between paving stones on a patio.
Propagation Small, non-flowering shoots can be easily rooted into sandy compost, or the whole plant can be divided.
Use Makes a sweetly scented lawn; the flowers can be dried and used in pot-pourris.
Others The true lawn chamomile is *Anthemis*

nobilis 'Treneague', which never flowers. The plants grow on small runners, which root where they touch the soil and slowly grow to make a highly scented, green carpet that will stay close to the ground. The other forms of chamomile are seldom so attractive – German chamomile (*Matricaria chamomilla*) is an annual grown for the single, daisy-like flowers, which are used for making tea; the common chamomile (*A. nobilis*) is a perennial with scented foliage and white daisy-like flowers that can be dried for use in pot-pourris and teas.

CHAMOMILE, DYER'S
Anthemis tinctoria (Compositae)
Perennial shrub.   see page 78

Origins Europe.
Ultimate size 3 ft × 2 ft (90 × 60 cm).
Soil Ordinary.
Sun/shade Sun.
Description Usually grown for the striking, yellow, daisy-like flowers, rather than as a plant for dying, dyer's chamomile can make a splendid splash of colour in the garden. The plant needs a good trim in October when the flowers have died down. The leaves are finely divided and remain on the plant all year.
Position A good spot plant to go toward the front of a sunny border, or at a point that can be seen in the distance against a dark background.
Propagation Easily grown from seed, it will flower in the same year if sown in early February. Cuttings can be taken in spring or the roots can be divided.

Use A traditional dye plant.
Others There are several garden forms of dyer's chamomile – 'E. C. Buxton' has lemon-yellow flowers, 'Grallagh Gold' has deep gold flowers, and 'Wargrave Variety' has soft cream flowers.

CHERVIL
Anthriscus cerefolium (Umbelliferae)
Annual.

Origins Native to Asia and eastern Europe.
Ultimate size 18 × 6in (45 × 15cm).
Soil Rich, moist.
Sun/shade Partial shade.
Description Finely cut, bright green leaves, running quickly to flower and seed. Toward the end of the plant's life the leaves turn first mauve and then brownish-red.
Position The feathery foliage looks delicate against the background of a sturdier plant, which will also provide light shade. It is an ideal container herb and it also makes a very good and attractive indoor plant.
Propagation Chervil seeds need to be fresh – they will then germinate quickly. As chervil runs very quickly to seed it should be sown in succession every two weeks to ensure a continuous supply.
Use An ingredient in *fines herbes*, together with chives, tarragon, and parsley. It is also good in scrambled eggs and omelettes and looks very pretty when used as a garnish for soups. A freshly tossed green salad is enhanced by a generous sprinkling of chervil.
Others There is no substitute.

CHIVES
Allium schoenoprasum (Liliaceae)
Perennial bulbs. see page 42

Origins   Cool parts of Europe.
Ultimate size   1 × 1ft (30 × 30cm).
Soil   Rich, loamy.
Sun/shade   Will tolerate most conditions, but needs some sun.
Description   Chives, with their grass-like, onion-flavoured leaves and pretty, purple flowers, are usually grown in the kitchen garden, but why not grow them in an herbaceous border? They flower prolifically in late May and, if the dead flowers are removed immediately, will give another crop of flowers in late summer. The flowers themselves have a slight onion flavour, which makes them even more attractive to use in cooking, and they look particularly pretty when grown in association with white sweet rocket.
Position   A good plant for growing at the front of a border, or it will make a very pretty edging plant alongside a path.
Propagation   Chives can readily be grown from seed and take about six months to reach a size suitable for cutting. Very large clumps can be split into several smaller clumps and replanted where required.
Use   The grass-like leaves with a mild onion flavour are used chopped into salads, soups, etc. Shred a few flowers into a salad for colour and extra flavour.
Others   There are a number of alliums, varying in height from 6in (15cm) to 3ft (1m); the flowers vary in colour from pinks to purples, white, yellows, and blues. *Allium schoenoprasum* 'Forcaste' grows slightly larger than the usual chives and has attractive pink flowers. The garlic chives (*A. tuberosum*) have flat leaves that have a strong taste of garlic and are delicious chopped into a salad – the flowers are white and come in late summer. Wild garlic (*A. ursinum*), often seen growing in woods and shady hedgerows, has broad, bright green leaves with a very pungent garlic scent and white flowers in early spring. Not all the wild garlics are edible.

COMFREY, DWARF
Symphytum grandiflorum (Boraginacae)
Perennial. see page 42

Origins   Europe and Asia.
Ultimate size   1ft (30cm) × unlimited spread.
Soil   Ordinary, moist.
Sun/shade   Full sun or partial shade.
Description   Hairy, dark green leaves almost all year, with an abundance of small yellow-pink flowers from early spring through the summer. It can be ruthlessly clipped back if it grows too fast or spreads too far, and unwanted leaves can be composted. They break down quickly and make a good rich mulch for the garden.
Position   Areas of waste garden that need ground cover that looks pretty as well as controlling weeds or covering something like a manhole. Dwarf comfrey will grow very happily in the gentle shade of trees such as silver birch where little else will thrive.
Propagation   Easily divided in the autumn or spring; simply replant the rooted pieces as required.

Use An excellent ground-cover plant.

Others The comfrey family is vast – some grow to several feet, while the dwarf comfries are low-growing. The flowers vary in colour, from pink (*Symphytum rubrum*), to purple or white (*S. officinale*), to bright blue (*S. caucasicum*). There are variegated varieties of both the dwarf and tall forms. The leaves of *S. officinale* may be chopped up and used in salads or cooked in the same way as spinach.

CORIANDER

Coriandrum sativum (Umbelliferae)
Annual.

Origins Native to eastern Europe and Mediterranean regions.

Ultimate size 12 × 6in (30 × 15cm).

Soil Rich, well-drained.

Sun/shade Sun.

Description Feathery, bright green leaves that, in their juvenile form, are very similar to those of French parsley. The pretty, pink flowers that produce the delicious seeds follow when the plant is about eight weeks old.

Position A useful herb for container growing; it can be grown as an indoor plant but its scent may be found unpleasant.

Propagation Coriander is grown from seed, which should be sown thinly, because each seed will produce two seedlings. Thin out the seedlings as soon as they are large enough to handle. Pinch out any flower heads that form in the first few weeks; after that allow them to develop, and when the seeds are brown and ripe, collect them, dry them off, and store them to use in cooking or for future sowings.

Use Coriander leaves have a very distinctive flavour, most often associated with Asian cooking. They can be used as a substitute for parsley, although they have a quite different and slightly acrid flavour. The seeds, when ground, have a sweet, spicy perfume and flavour and go well with fruit dishes and chutneys.

Others 'Wild' coriander is not truly wild; it is a garden escapee.

COTTON LAVENDER

Santolina chamaecyparissus (Compositae)
Evergreen, perennial shrub.   see pages 35 and 51

Origins Southern Europe and north Africa.

Ultimate size 2ft × 1ft 6in (60 × 45cm).

Soil Light, well-drained.

Sun/shade Full sunshine.

Description With its silver-grey foliage, cotton lavender makes an excellent small hedge. Hard clipping in the late spring encourages new growth low down the stems and keeps a neat shape while discouraging the somewhat uninteresting yellow, button flowers from appearing too early and spoiling the lines of the hedge.

Position An excellent plant to make a small hedge or add a spot of silver against a dark background.

Propagation Take cuttings of non-flowering wood in early summer, and root in a peat and sand mix. Plant the rooted cuttings the following autumn or spring.

Use The cut stems keep well in flower arrangements. Dried leaves are often used in insect-repellent sachets.

Others There are several varieties of santolina with silver foliage – *Santolina serratifolia* has finely cut foliage with bright, yellow, button flowers, *S. neapolitana* has pale cream flowers, and *S. nana* grows to about 1ft (30cm) and has gold-yellow flowers.

COWSLIP
Primula veris (Primulaceae)
Perennial. see page 42

Origins Northern and central Europe.
Ultimate size 12 × 6in (30 × 15cm).
Soil Open and sandy, with added leaf mould.
Sun/shade Some sun with dappled shade.
Description Soft green leaves up to $3\frac{1}{2}$in (8cm) long, with clusters of very pretty, yellow flowers on stalks rising up to 7in (16cm). The clumps slowly increase over the years.
Position Cowslips need some dappled shade and grow most happily among other plants at the front of a border or in long grass in a wild garden.
Propagation Cowslips will self-seed readily if the seed heads are given time to ripen before being cut. A large clump can be split into plantlets.
Use In the past the flowers were used to make wine and a syrup or crystallized to make cake decorations; today they are mainly decorative. The flowers were formerly used also as a cosmetic and, medically, in an infusion or mixed with wine, as a sedative. The roots were used as a treatment for bronchitis and coughs.

Others Other forms of cowslips are available – there are varieties with flowers of various shades of orange, rusty red, and cream, most having the delicate scent of the parent. They cross-pollinate easily with other primulas and so may not come true to the parent. The primrose (*Primula vulgaris*) is a shade-loving plant, with single, pale yellow flowers on a single stalk. The oxlip (*P. elatior*) is a hybrid between cowslip and primrose and produces smaller flowers than the primrose on a multiple head like the cowslip.

CRANESBILL
Geranium macrorrhizum (Geraniaceae)
Semi-evergreen perennial. see page 46

Origins Southeastern Europe.
Ultimate size 12–15 × 18in (30–38 × 45cm).
Soil Ordinary, well-drained.
Sun/shade Sun or partial shade.
Description The green leaves give off a strong perfume when touched, and turn a fine red in the autumn. The flowers are usually of pink or white, and borne most of the summer. The plant makes excellent ground cover, spreading fast.
Position Looks good in any spot in the garden, but is best towards the front of a border, where it can be brushed in passing to release the stunning scent. Especially successful when grown in conjunction with pinks and perennial salvias.
Propagation Divide the clumps during the autumn and also the spring and replant in the garden as required.
Use An attractive border plant with very good

autumn colour. The leaves could be dried and added to pot-pourris.

Others The geranium family is enormous, though few of its members have such a strong perfume – they are all hardy herbaceous perennials, with small, often brightly coloured flowers of pinks, blues, whites, and purples that last most of the summer.

CURRY PLANT
Helichrysum angustifolium (Compositae)
Evergreen perennial. see pages 35 and 42

Origins Southern Europe.
Ultimate size 2ft × 1ft 6in (60 × 45cm).
Soil Open, well-drained.
Sun/shade Full sun in a sheltered position.
Description The curry plant has short, spiky, silver leaves, which on a damp day release their evocative curry smell. A gentle prune in the spring, midsummer, and autumn will help keep a curry plant in good shape, as it will not take happily to a heavy clip once a year. The yellow flowers are very dull to look at, and are best pinched off as they appear.
Position A very good plant for a corner, set against a dark leaf plant. Remaining 'ever-silver' all year it will lighten any corner. If you loathe the smell of curry, it's probably best to relegate the curry plant to a distant spot. If it pleases you, it is a lovely plant to have towards the front of a border, where the scent can be appreciated in passing.
Propagation Cuttings of semi-ripe wood taken in midsummer will root readily in a sandy soil. Transplant to their final position the following spring.

Use This plant will not produce a hot curry, but if a hint of flavour is all that is needed, a few leaves chopped up into the dish should do the trick.
Others The family is large, with *Helichrysum plicatum* having long, silver, needle-like leaves and the same faint, curry scent. *H. splendidum* has attractive silver-blue foliage, but no scent.

DILL
Anethum graveolens (Umbelliferae)
Annual.

Origins Grows wild in North and South America and in Europe.
Ultimate size 2 × 1ft (60 × 30cm).
Soil Ordinary, well-drained.
Sun/shade Sun.
Description A tall, feathery herb with soft blue-green foliage on a single stem and heads of yellow flowers. Dill is similar in appearance to fennel, and the two should not be grown too near to one another or they may cross-pollinate and produce 'dennel'.
Position A decorative plant for the border, it should be given a site out of the wind in full sun. It makes a good container herb and can be grown indoors.
Propagation Dill should be grown from seed sown in early spring. As it will run to seed quickly, it should be sown little and often.
Use A great culinary herb, with no hint of aniseed, the chopped leaves will enhance the flavour of any salad or any vegetable. The subtle, mild flavour is excellent with fish.
Others The delicate flavour of dill is unique, so as

a culinary herb it is, strictly, irreplaceable. Fennel is the nearest equivalent in kitchen and garden.

ELDER, PURPLE

Sambucus nigra 'Purpurea' (Caprifoliaceae)
Shrub or small tree.   see page 45

Origins Europe.
Ultimate size 13 × 10ft (4 × 3m).
Soil Fertile.
Sun/shade Sun or partial shade – the colour of the leaves will remain darker if grown in part shade.
Description This elder is less of a problem to the gardener than the common type as it does not self-seed so readily. The purple, pinnate leaves make a wonderful show in summer, while the flowers of white flushed with pink, appearing in late May, are quite exquisite. A small crop of black elderberries will usually appear in the autumn and last until eaten by the birds.
Position With its dark leaves, purple elder makes a quite lovely backdrop for the silver plants in the garden. It is best planted at the back of a border, as it will make substantial growth in a season. Prune back to about 3ft (1m) in the late autumn to maintain the shrub to a reasonable size and a good shape.
Propagation Cuttings taken from hard wood in early autumn will root readily in a nursery bed. Plant in their ultimate positions the following autumn.
Use As with all the elders, the flowers can be used to make a very potent 'champagne', and they have excellent properties when used in natural cosmetics; the berries are used for jams or wines.
Others There is a wide range of very beautiful elders with golden leaves, variegated leaves, and finely cut green or gold leaves. A variety from North America has red fruit. All have the traditional heads of scented florets.

ELECAMPANE

Inula helenium (Compositae)
Perennial.   see page 45

Origins Asia.
Ultimate size 10 × 3ft (3 × 1m).
Soil Moisture-retentive.
Sun/shade Full sun.
Description A statuesque plant with large leaves that are wonderful in early summer, spreading about 8in (20cm) across and 24in (60cm) tall; with the sun behind they look almost translucent. The plant then goes to flower, getting taller every day, ending in August with waving heads of dandelion-like flowers. It needs staking by about mid-July as it is likely to be felled by strong winds.
Position Best towards the back of a border, it looks good planted in partnership with soapwort (*Saponaria officinalis*) and *Salvia horminum*.
Propagation It is best to divide the clumps during the winter and replant as required. It is quite possible to grow elecampane from seed, but germination is erratic and the plant may become invasive if not tended carefully.
Use The roots were formerly used to make a cough medicine. It is now best employed as a piece of living sculpture in the garden.
Others A large family of 200 perennials, some growing large, while others – such as *Inula acaulis* –

only reach 2–4in (5–10cm) and so are suitable for a rock garden.

EVENING PRIMROSE
Oenothera biennis (Onagraceae)
Biennial.   see page 63

Origins   North America, where it now grows wild in many places.
Ultimate size   3 × 1ft (90 × 30cm).
Soil   Any soil.
Sun/shade   Sun.
Description   In the first year, long, tapering leaves up to about 6in (15cm) tall rise out of a thick rosette. The second year large, bright yellow, saucer-shaped flowers open all the way up the tapering stems. These are attractive to insects and are especially beautiful in the evening when they release their perfume and the flowers stand out in gold discs against the fading night light, looking almost phosphorescent.
Position   Growing quite tall, they are best planted towards the back of a border, and look especially good when planted against a dark background.
Propagation   Liable to self-seed prolifically, the seeds are slow and erratic to germinate artificially. It is best to allow seedlings to grow where the seeds drop, and then transplant to the final position in late spring or early autumn.
Use   This plant has a valuable place in the herb garden. Not only is it of much current interest for the medicinal qualities of the seeds, but the whole plant is edible in various recipes; young roots can be boiled or pickled and eaten as a vegetable – tasting rather like parsnip – while the young leaves can be added to salads.
Others   The evening primrose family is made up of about eighty species. Most have yellow saucer-shaped flowers with a faint scent, although there are a few with white or pale pink flowers. Some are perennial or annual. *Oenothera fruticosa*, a perennial with very attractive coppery foliage and yellow flowers, grows to about 2ft (60cm) tall and is a most attractive plant for a small herb garden.

FENNEL, BRONZE
Foeniculum vulgare 'Purpureum' (Umbelliferae)
Perennial.   see page 56

Origins   Mediterranean regions.
Ultimate size   1ft (30cm) × up to 6ft (2m).
Soil   Very well-drained.
Sun/shade   Full sun.
Description   Bronze fennel has very striking foliage, soft and fluffy when young, which fades a bit as the season progresses. The flat, yellow flowers appear in late summer, and are popular with butterflies and bees. If left to die naturally with the onset of winter, the fennel skeleton provides wonderful shapes in the beds when there is little else to see.
Position   Ultimately becoming a large plant, fennel is best grown towards the back of an herbaceous border. The colour blends particularly well with the soft shades of sages and lavenders and the structure contrasts well with that of angelica.
Propagation   Once established, fennel will self-seed readily around the herb garden – a few sessions with a hoe will weed out the surplus seedlings. A

clump that has got too large can be split in the spring.

Use A quite beautiful structure plant for the garden, fennel is wonderful for flower arrangements. The stalks add tremendous flavour to barbequed meats or may be used in marinades. The leaves are good chopped finely and sprinkled on to salads and oily fish dishes.

Others Green fennel (*Foeniculum vulgare*) grows wild in southern Europe and can be used in the same ways as bronze fennel. The sweet fennel (*F.v.* var *dulce*), with a swollen bulb at its base, is an annual, cultivated quite differently, with a strongly aniseed flavour. The bulbs are delicious sliced thinly, sautéd in lemon juice until tender, and served with grilled fish or steaks.

FOXGLOVE

Digitalis purpurea (Scrophulariaceae)
Biennial.   see page 45

Origins Western Europe including Great Britain.
Ultimate size 3–5ft (1–1.5m).
Soil Ordinary garden soil that stays moist in summer.
Sun/shade Partial shade.
Description The common English foxglove may live longer than two years under perfect conditions, but will usually only form a large rosette of felty leaves the first year, throwing up a slender spire of pink or white flowers in the second summer. The flowers are bell-shaped and tubular, resembling the fingers of a glove; the lower lip is usually marked with dark spots.

Position Often found growing wild in shady woodland, or on banks and under hedges, foxgloves like shade and grow well in wild, woodland gardens or under the protection of a tall hedge.
Propagation Foxgloves will self-seed readily, if the flower head is allowed to remain *in situ* while the seeds ripen. Alternatively, sow fresh seed very thinly outside in the late spring, thin out the seedlings, and plant in their final positions in the autumn.
Use The leaves are used for the extraction of the drug digitalin (one of the most important cardiac stimulants), but for this use they must be from the pure, dull pink form rather than any of the ornamental varieties.
Others There is a very beautiful white flowering form of the wild foxglove, which makes a wonderful garden plant – *Digitalis purpurea alba*. Several hybrid varieties have also been introduced – *D. purpurea* 'Excelsior' grows to 6ft (2m) and has flowers held horizontally; *D. purpurea* 'Foxy' grows to only 2ft 6in (75cm) but, with its wide range of flower colours, is very suitable for cutting.

FOXGLOVE, YELLOW

Digitalis lutea (Scrophulariaceae)
Short-lived perennial.

Origins Southwest Europe and northwest Africa.
Ultimate size 3 × 1ft (90 × 30cm).
Soil Ordinary garden soil that remains damp during the summer.
Sun/shade Partial shade.
Description The small, yellow-flowered foxglove has a gentle beauty that is quite different from that of

the wild foxglove. It has shiny green, heavily veined leaves and pale yellow flowers, about ¾in (2cm) long, which hang on tapering spires about 3ft (1m) tall. It flowers from May to July and, if cut down without setting seed, will grow on to make larger clumps for the following year.

Position A splendid plant for growing toward the front of a shady border.

Propagation Easily grown from seed, *Digitalis lutea* will self-seed very readily if left alone after flowering and not cut down until the early autumn.

Use A pretty garden plant with ancient herbal uses.

Others This is just one of about thirty varieties of foxglove – the common, wild plants with purple or white flowers that are so splendid in a wild garden setting. *D. lanata* has attractive soft, hairy, white flowers and bright green leaves; *D. ferruginea* grows to about 5ft (1.5m) and has brown-red flowers opening in July.

GERANIUM 'LADY PLYMOUTH'
Pelargonium 'Lady Plymouth' (Geraniaceae)
Perennial sub-shrub.

Origins South Africa.
Ultimate size Up to 3ft × 1ft 6in (90 × 45cm).
Soil Ordinary, well-drained, garden soil.
Sun/shade Full sun.
Description A spreading, branching plant with palmate, deeply lobed, scented leaves that are a pale green with cream variegation. The scent is hard to describe – a cross between lemon, rose, and balsam. Small, pink flowers are borne all summer.

Position Best grown in a large flower pot, perhaps on a patio or beside a path, where the scent can be appreciated in passing. It is possible to plant these geraniums out for the summer once all frost is past, but they must be lifted before the first frosts of autumn.

Propagation Take cuttings from non-flowering branches in the early autumn. Overwinter the cuttings in a frost-free environment and transplant into large pots in the following spring. Pinch out the growing tips to encourage bushy growth.

Use The leaves give off their lovely scent to anyone passing who brushes the foliage. They dry well and are used in pot-pourris.

Others There are many different scented-leaf geraniums. Several have variegated foliage – *Pelargonium crispum* 'Variegatum' has small, cream, variegated, crinkly foliage with a strong, lemon scent; *P. × fragrans* 'Variegatum' has small, cream, variegated leaves with a hint of nutmeg in the perfume.

GERANIUM, ROSE
Pelargonium graveolens (Geraniaceae)
Perennial sub-shrub.

Origins South Africa.
Ultimate size Up to 3ft × 1ft 6in (90 × 45cm).
Soil Ordinary, well-drained.
Sun/shade Full sun.
Description A spreading, branching plant with palmate, slightly hairy, deeply lobed, scented leaves. The scent is sometimes described as lemon, sometimes rose, but is not easy to define. The pale pink

flowers are borne all summer and into the autumn.

Position Must be placed where the leaves can be brushed in passing to release the magical scent. In winter, *Pelargonium graveolens* can be brought into the house, where it should thrive, provided that the light is fairly good.

Propagation Take cuttings from non-flowering tips in the early autumn. Overwinter in a frost-free environment and pot on into larger pots in the spring.

Use The scented leaves can be used to make the most delicious ice-cream or sorbet – make a sugar syrup with a cup of water to a spoonful of sugar, bring to the boil, and plunge a handful of leaves into the syrup. Cover, and leave to cool. Strain off the syrup and use it to flavour an ice-cream made with a standard recipe.

Others Among the many other scented geraniums are 'Attar of Roses', with soft, rounded leaves, pale-pink flowers, and a strong rose scent; 'Prince of Orange', with dark green, crisp leaves and a scent of orange; *P. odoratissimum*, with round, soft leaves and a scent of apples; 'Filicifolium', with slightly sticky, very finely divided, palmate leaves and a strong scent of balsam; and the spicy *P. × fragans*.

Description A hardy, small shrub with glossy, dark green foliage. Spikes of pink flowers come in late summer. Cut the plant lightly back to tidy it in the autumn, then cut hard back in late spring to keep the plant neat.

Position The germander makes a very good, small, neat hedge to edge a garden or form a part of a knot. As a single specimen plant it is very successful in a small bed alongside a patio or in conjunction with a brighter foliage plant such as a golden marjoram.

Propagation Semi-hard cuttings can be taken in early summer and rooted in a sandy mix. Plant out into their final positions the following spring. Germander grown from seed is often a laxer, more floppy plant than its parents.

Use A traditional, small hedging plant; the leaves have been used in herbal medicines.

Others Occasionally a variegated leaf form will appear with cream splashes on the leaves. This is pretty but seldom makes good strong growth. *Teucrium fruticans* is a less hardy perennial with large, silver leaves and blue flowers, needing a very sheltered spot. *T. fruticans* 'Azureum' is similar, with very dark blue flowers, but is only half-hardy.

GERMANDER
Teucrium chamaedrys (Labiatae)
Evergreen perennial.   see pages 35 and 46

Origins Europe.
Ultimate size 1 × 1ft (30 × 30cm).
Soil Light, well-drained.
Sun/shade Full sun.

GOAT'S RUE, WHITE
Galega officinalis 'Alba' (Leguminosae)
Perennial.   see page 35

Origins Native to Italy and Asia Minor.
Ultimate size 4ft 6in × 2ft (140 × 60cm).
Soil Well-drained.
Sun/shade Sun or light shade.

Description The leaves are pale green, vetch-like, with white, pea-like flowers in late summer.
Position It makes a very striking plant when grown with verbascums or large geraniums. Growing tall, it is best planted towards the back of a border, where the stakes that may be needed by late summer are hidden.
Propagation Divide the clumps in the winter and replant *in situ*. Plants grown from seed may not be true to their parent.
Use Said to help increase milk production in mammals, the fresh juice clots milk and has been used in cheese production.
Others The more usual form has pale purple flowers, while, of the named varieties, 'Her Majesty' is a soft lilac-purple and 'Lady Wilson' mauve and cream.

HEARTSEASE
Viola tricolor (Violaceae)
Annual or short-lived perennial. see page 77

Origins European native, found wild in fields, on wastelands, or in hedgerows.
Ultimate size 6in × 6in (15cm × 15cm).
Soil Acidic, rich, damp.
Sun/shade Sun.
Description A parent of the modern pansy, heartsease often has rather straggly growth. The petals are small and, as the species name recognizes, three-coloured. As the herb hybridizes readily, there are many flower varieties – almost black, all purple, almost all yellow, or mixed in varying proportions.
Position A pretty plant to place at the front of a border. It will self-seed with vigour and appear in the most unexpected places – a favourite is between cracks in paving, where it can look quite delightful.
Propagation Grow from seed sown in the spring, or allow it to self-seed.
Use Formerly used as a blood-purifying agent and as a lotion to help heal wounds.
Others There are very many forms of heartsease and pansy, with a myriad different colour patterns.

HONEYSUCKLE, AMERICAN
Lonicera × americana (Caprifoliaceae)
Climber. see page 46

Origins Sometimes found wild in southern Europe.
Ultimate size 12 × 12ft (4 × 4m).
Soil Ordinary, well-drained, enriched with humus.
Sun/shade Sun or part shade, best with the roots planted in shade.
Description A strong-growing deciduous climber with grey-green leaves. The flowers, opening in June, have dark-red buds that open to a soft cream colour and are very highly scented.
Position A good climber for a wall or fence or to cover the upright of a pergola. Best planted where the wonderful scent can be appreciated. This honeysuckle looks stunning when planted close to the all-heal valerian (*Valeriana officinalis*). Thin out old wood as required after flowering.
Propagation Cuttings taken in midsummer and planted in sandy rooting beds. Plant out finally the following spring.

Use Grow on a wall where the wonderful scent can be appreciated.
Others There are many honeysuckles – evergreen, deciduous, climbers, and shrubs. *Lonicera standishii* is a semi-evergreen shrub with sweetly scented cream flowers from November to March. *L. japonica* 'Halliana' is an evergreen with cream, scented flowers all summer. *L. syringantha* is a large, deciduous shrub with sweetly scented, pink flowers in May and June.

HOP, GOLDEN
Humulus lupulus 'Aureus' (Cannabidaceae)
Climber. see page 50

Origins Native to temperate areas of Europe.
Ultimate size 30 × 12ft (10 × 4m).
Soil Damp, humus-rich.
Sun/shade Roots shaded by other plants, heads happy in full sun.
Description A climber with very rough stems that rapidly climb clockwise up anything they touch. The flowers, produced in late summer, are greenish-yellow clusters of papery bracts. The bracts ripen in the autumn to brown, cone-like shells, which have a strong, heady perfume; these are the 'fuggles' used in brewing.
Position A wonderful plant for covering in summer a dull fence, a pergola, or an old tree stump. When trained over a post or wigwam of canes in the centre of a bed, it immediately adds important structure to a herb garden.
Propagation Grow from cuttings taken in the early spring.

Use The dried flowers are used in beer making and, because of their soporific scent, in 'sleep pillows'. The young shoots may be cut and eaten like asparagus in early spring. The leaves, after parboiling to remove their bitterness, can be used to flavour soups. **Warning:** hop pollen causes, in a few people, contact dermatitis
Others The wild, green hop is the form normally used in commercial beer making. The annual, variegated hop (*Humulus japonica*) makes an interesting summer covering for a wall, fence, or pillar.

HYSSOP, PINK
Hyssopus officinalis 'Roseus' (Labiatae)
Semi-evergreen, perennial shrub. see page 48

Origins Native to central and southern Europe.
Ultimate size 2 × 1ft (60 × 30cm).
Soil Light, well-drained.
Sun/shade Full sun.
Description A small shrub with short, spiky, dark green, very aromatic leaves. The bright pink flowers appear in July and are in great favour with bees because of the abundance of nectar.
Position Towards the front of a border, hyssop looks wonderful when grown in combination with musk mallow, bergamot, and catmint.
Propagation May be grown from cuttings taken in early summer or from seed sown in spring, although plants grown from seed may not produce the same flower colour as the parent plant.
Use The dried flowering tops and leaves are used in herbal medicines to stimulate the appetite and to reduce perspiration. Small amounts of chopped

leaves are good to flavour soups and stews.

Others The usual hyssop has bright blue flowers, but others are found with white or purple flowers.

HYSSOP, ROCK
Hyssopus aristatus (Labiatae)
Semi-evergreen perennial shrub.

Origins Native to central and southern Europe.
Ultimate size 1 × 1ft (30 × 30cm).
Soil Light, well-drained.
Sun/shade Full sun.
Description A small shrub with short, bright green, spiky leaves and very pretty, dark blue flowers in midsummer.
Position Toward the front of the herb border, in combination with thymes and other small herbs, or it may be used to make a low hedge around a bed.
Propagation From cuttings taken in early summer.
Use The leaves may be chopped and added to food in place of pink hyssop.
Others The commoner, non-dwarf species is *Hyssopus officinalis*, for one variety of which see previous entry.

LADY'S MANTLE
Alchemilla vulgaris (Rosaceae)
Perennial.   see pages 37 and 51

Origins Northern Europe and pastures of mountainous areas.

Ultimate size 1 × 1ft (30 × 30cm).
Soil Deep, loamy, with no lime.
Sun/shade Slightly shaded by other plants.
Description Soft, branched stems bearing pale green, softly hairy, round leaves, with masses of fluffy, yellow flowers in summer. Most attractive after rainfall when the leaves are covered by drops of water.
Position Towards the front of a border or along the edge of a path where the soft shape can break up the hard edge.
Propagation Self-seeds readily, so it is best to dig up the seedlings in the following summer.
Use Traditionally a wound herb to promote healing, lady's mantle has also been used to treat menstrual problems. It makes an excellent garden plant and keeps well in flower arrangements.
Others The large-growing *Alchemilla mollis* is more usually grown and is very prolific. The attractive *A. alpina* has small leaves edged with silver.

LAVENDER 'HIDCOTE'
Lavandula angustifolia (syn. *L. spica*) 'Hidcote' (Labiatae)
Perennial shrub.   see page 52

Origins Native to Mediterranean regions.
Ultimate size 2 × 2ft (60 × 60cm).
Soil Not too rich, well-drained.
Sun/shade Full sun.
Description A compact plant with spiky, grey leaves, strongly aromatic, and short, dark purple flowers in midsummer.
Position An excellent plant to make a small, neat

hedge to border a path or put on or alongside a wall. Lavenders also make good specimen plants to place around old-fashioned roses or among other herbs.

Propagation By cuttings taken from non-flowering, semi-mature wood in August.

Use The dried flowers are frequently used in pot-pourris or, on their own, in lavender bags. Lavender oil is a stimulant and may be used to prevent vertigo and fainting. Dried lavender flowers are often found as an ingredient in Provençal herb mixes. An infusion of lavender and other herbs, such as thyme, rosemary, balm and eau-de-Cologne mint, can be used to make a relaxing aromatic bath.

Others The lavender family is vast – many seedlings have arisen to give a large range of size, shape, and flower colour. Purples range from washed-out to very dark, some grow to 3ft (1m) in spread and height, while others stay small and tidy. The old-fashioned varieties of lavender seem to be making a comeback – *Lavandula angustifolia* 'Grappenhall' grows to about 3ft (1m) with long, pale flower heads; *L. pinnata* 'Seal,' originating at Margaret Brownlow's Herb Farm, grows tall, is very free-flowering, and is excellent for cutting and drying; Dutch lavender (*L. vera*) is a smaller, more compact plant with mid-purple flowers. The lavender most commonly grown in the Mediterranean regions is French lavender (*L. stoechas*), which has a very strong perfume and interesting flower heads topped by dark purple bracts; there is also a white flowering form of *L. stoechas*. There are several half-hardy lavenders with interesting leaf and flower shapes that have to be kept frost free in winter – *L. multifida* has very soft, hairy foliage and purple flowers; and the very beautiful *L. viridis* has soft green foliage and pale purple flowers.

LAVENDER 'LODDON PINK'
Lavandula latifolia 'Loddon Pink' (Labiatae)
Perennial shrub.   see page 52

Origins Garden form grown in temperate regions.

Ultimate size 2ft × 1ft 6in (60 × 45cm).

Soil Well-drained.

Sun/Shade Full sun.

Description A tidy shrub with spiky, grey leaves and short, compact heads of pale pink flowers.

Position A good variety for a small hedge, or to use as a mass planting scheme, perhaps under old roses.

Use The flowers dry well, but are not very decorative because of their pale colour.

Others There are several forms of pink-flowered lavender, including 'Jean Davis' and 'Hidcote Pink', but all are very similar in growing habit and colour. White-flowering lavenders are also found – *Lavandula angustifolia* 'Alba' grows to about 3ft (1m) with tall spikes of white flowers; *L. multifida* 'Nana Alba' is a dwarf white lavender, growing to only 1ft (30cm), bearing short spikes of highly scented white flowers all summer.

LEMON BALM, VARIEGATED
Melissa officinalis 'Variegata' (Labiatae)
Perennial.   see page 37

Origins Native to southern Europe; largely garden escape elsewhere.

Ultimate size 3 × 2ft (90 × 60cm).
Soil Rich, moist.
Sun/shade Sun with some shade.
Description Dark green leaves with strong, gold variegation round the edges, lemon-scented when crushed. Hairy stems and leaves, with tiny white flowers in the leaf axils.
Position Better grown towards the centre of a border, but lovely if it is possible to have a clump near a path, where the leaves can be brushed on passing.
Propagation Take cuttings in the summer, or divide the clump in the autumn and replant as required. Self-sown seedlings are unlikely to have the variegation and so are best hoed out.
Use The fresh leaves can be used to make an aromatic tea for the treatment of minor gastric disorders. Dried leaves may be used in pot-pourris and aromatic mixtures.
Others The usual lemon balm has rather uninteresting green leaves and seeds itself without hesitation. A golden form is weaker than the type.

LEMON VERBENA
Aloysia triphylla syn. *Lippia citriodora*
(Verbenaceae)
Perennial shrub.   see page 76

Origins Native to parts of South America.
Ultimate size 6 × 3ft (2 × 1m).
Soil Well-drained, ordinary.
Sun/shade Full sun.
Description Pale to mid-green lanceolate leaves with a very strong lemon scent when crushed. Tiny pale flowers in late summer in panicles 3–4in (7.5–10cm) long. Can be clipped and trained to make a standard shrub.
Position Best grown in containers that can be kept in a frost-free greenhouse or conservatory in winter. If space is available, plant out in late May and allow to grow naturally where it can be crushed on passing to release the wonderful perfume. Dig up again at the first frost and re-pot, keeping almost dry during the winter. In very sheltered gardens, lemon verbena may survive if planted close to the foot of a south-facing wall.
Propagation In midsummer take cuttings of half-ripe wood, inserting into a sandy mix. When rooted, pot and overwinter in a frost-free place.
Use Lemon verbena, with its quite delicious scent, dries wonderfully – use for pleasant teas and add to pot-pourris and scented sachets. It is said to have a slightly sedative effect. In its native South America, oil of lemon verbena was used to scent fingerbowls at banquets.
Others This is one of the best-known of all scented-leaf plants, but many other plants can be grown, given a frost-free enviroment, that also have scented foliage – balm of Gilead, *Cedronella triphylla*, the scented-leaf geraniums, and myrtle (*Myrtus communis*) to list only a few.

LOOSESTRIFE, PURPLE
Lythrum salicaria (Lythraceae)
Perennial   see page 54

Origins Native to Europe and western Asia.
Ultimate size 8 × 3ft (2.4 × 1m).

Soil   Ordinary, damp.

Sun/shade   Sun or semi-shade.

Description   A very tall plant with bright purple flowers closely packed in 9–12in (20–30cm) spires in late summer.

Position   It makes a striking addition to a border when planted alongside a silver artemisia (*Artemisia ludoviciana* 'Silver Queen') or the tall *A. lactiflora*.

Propagation   Will grow readily from seed sown in the spring, or a large clump may be divided. Cuttings may be taken in spring. It may become invasive.

Use   Once used in the tanning of leather, the plant is occasionally still used in European folk medicine as an astringent and antidiarrhoeal decoction.

Others   Named varieties of loosestrife are available with especially attractive flowers – 'Dropmore' is purple, 'Lady Sackville', bright rose-pink, 'The Beacon', deep rose-crimson.

LOVAGE
Levisticum officinale (Umbelliferae)
Perennial.   see page 54

Origins   South European native, naturalized in the eastern United States.

Ultimate size   9 × 3ft (3 × 1m).

Soil   Most soils except heavy clay.

Sun/shade   Sun.

Description   A tall-growing herb with round, hollow stems. The leaves have a strong, yeasty taste, and should be used when young and tender. The small, yellow flowers appear in midsummer.

Position   Best planted at the back of a border, it looks good growing next to soapwort (*Saponaria officinalis*) and queen of the meadow with their contrasting leaf shapes.

Propagation   The root can be split and replanted in the autumn after the foliage has died down. Fresh seed germinates readily.

Use   Young leaves are good finely chopped and sprinkled on to salads or with new potatoes.

Others   A very similar plant is Scots lovage (*Ligusticum scoticum*), which does not grow so tall, but may be used and eaten in the same ways. Another pot herb, alexanders (*Smyrnium olusatrum*), is similar in appearance, with large, green leaves and a yellow flower head.

MALLOW, WHITE MUSK
Malva moschata 'Alba' (Malvaceae)
Biennial or short-lived perennial.   see page 54

Origins   Europe.

Ultimate size   2 × 1ft (60 × 30cm).

Soil   Ordinary garden soil.

Sun/shade   Sun or partial shade.

Description   The deeply cut, bright green leaves have a slight musky scent when bruised. Spikes of white flowers with a very pale touch of pink in the centre have a delicate scent. Cut down in the autumn.

Position   Any position in a border will do justice to these beautiful plants, but a dark background will emphasize the delicate, white flowers.

Propagation   Readily self-seeding. The seeds can be sown in a greenhouse in spring, and the larger plants planted out in the autumn.

Use Modern herbal medicine has no use for the musk mallow, but that must not exclude it from the garden.

Others A pink-flowered musk mallow is also commonly found growing wild, and makes a wonderful garden plant when grown in conjunction with white-flowering plants. Other mallows include the marshmallow (*Althaea officinalis*), which grows up to 6ft (2m) and has pretty, pale pink flowers.

MARIGOLD, POT
Calendula officinalis (Compositae)
Annual. see page 56

Origins Southern Europe.
Ultimate size 1 × 1ft (30 × 30cm).
Soil Well-drained.
Sun/shade Full sun or partial shade.
Description The old-fashioned marigold has a mass of orange or yellow petals arranged round a central 'eye'. The leaves have a strong scent when crushed.
Position A must anywhere in the herb garden, marigolds can be placed anywhere in the border where colour is needed.
Propagation A self-seeding annual, which will survive right into the winter and start to germinate with the first ray of sunshine in the spring, marigolds will propagate themselves with no trouble.
Use Marigold petals make a salad look exquisite – tear off the petals and scatter them over the greenery. Add a few petals to a rice dish for a cheap saffron substitute. Marigold flowers dry well and make a colourful addition to pot-pourris.

Others The tagetes or African marigolds have no real place in the herb garden – they are not edible, nor do they smell good.

MARJORAM, COMPACT
Origanum vulgare 'Compactum' (Labiatae)
Perennial. see page 56

Origins Garden form of a wild plant found over most of Europe.
Ultimate size 7 × 12in (18 × 30cm).
Soil Well-drained, ordinary.
Sun/shade Best in full sun.
Description A neat compact plant with bright green leaves and pink flowers in midsummer.
Position A super little plant to place at the front of a border – best grouped in threes to make a larger clump.
Propagation The whole plant may be split and replanted in the early autumn or spring. Cuttings taken before flowering has started root easily in sandy soil.
Use A very strongly flavoured marjoram, this is excellent with pasta sauces and fish dishes, or sprinkled on to a barbeque to perfume the air.
Others The marjorams make up a fairly small species of aromatic half-hardy and hardy shrubs from the Mediterranean area. Some, such as *Origanum dictamnus*, have wonderful grey, hairy leaves with pretty pink flowers, while others, such as the sweet marjoram (*O. majorana*), are tender but have a sweetly scented flavour. The marjorams hybridize readily, so there are a number of varieties with the characteristics of several species.

MARJORAM, GOLDEN
Origanum vulgare 'Aureum' (Labiatae)
Perennial.   see page 59

Origins   Garden form of a wild plant found over most of Europe.
Ultimate size   15 × 24in (40 × 60cm).
Soil   Well-drained, ordinary.
Sun/shade   Best in full sun, though will grow in part shade.
Description   Bright yellow foliage spreading, in time, to make a large clump. If, in midsummer, the clump collapses and the centre opens out, trim back to ground level to allow fresh new growth to take over. Pretty, pale pink flowers rise above the foliage in late summer.
Position   A wonderful clump of colour towards the front of a border or in a bed alongside a patio. A tremendous colour combination is made by combining golden marjoram, pink bluebeard (*Salvia horminum*), *Artemisia* 'Old Warrior' and rue (*Ruta graveolens*).
Propagation   Golden marjoram self-seeds readily, so there will always be plenty of small plants dotted around the bed to move if required. An alternative method of increasing golden marjoram is to split the clump in the autumn and replant as required.
Use   With its strong flavour, golden marjoram is a good variety to use whenever fresh marjoram is called for.
Others   There are several forms of golden marjoram – one with tiny, curled gold leaves tends to scorch badly in bright sunshine. Golden-tipped marjoram has green leaves, splashed on the tips with gold, and is very pretty.

MARJORAM, SWEET
Origanum majorana (Labiatae)
Annual.

Origins   Native to eastern Mediterranean regions, used especially by the Greeks.
Ultimate size   12 × 6in (30 × 15cm).
Soil   Ordinary, well-drained.
Sun/shade   Full sun.
Description   A tender plant with highly scented, soft green leaves and small knots of white flowers in summer.
Position   Plant in the warmest and most sheltered spot in the garden, or grow in a container and keep it inside during the winter until all risk of frost has passed.
Propagation   Sow seeds thinly in late spring and prick out when large enough to handle. Sweet marjoram needs plenty of water during dry spells in summer.
Use   With its highly aromatic scent and flavour, sweet marjoram is a milder, but still spicy, alternative to oregano (*Origanum vulgare*, the wild marjoram). It is delicious when rubbed in to a joint of meat before roasting or when used to add flavour to pizzas and pasta sauces. Sweet marjoram can be used to make an interesting herb vinegar
Others   *O. onites*, the pot or French marjoram, is often included in a bouquet garni. Two more decorative varieties of oregano are *O. vulgare* 'Variegatum' and *O. vulgare* 'Compactum'.

MINT, EAU-DE-COLOGNE
Mentha × piperita nm. 'Citrata' (Labiatae)
Perennial.

Origins European native.
Ultimate size Height to 2ft (60cm).
Soil Rich, moist.
Sun/shade Partial shade.
Description A very attractive mint with dark green, purple-tinged stems and leaves. The leaves have a pleasing, fresh scent, described variously as lemon, eau-de-Cologne, bergamot or lavender. Formerly called *Mentha odorata*, which perhaps was more accurate. Whorls of purple-pink flowers in late summer.
Position A wild root runner, so should always be grown in a container such as a sunken bucket or surrounded by paving stones.
Propagation Split and replant the clumps of root in the autumn or spring.
Use The leaves may be dried and used to scent bath-herb mixtures and cosmetics. The leaves may also be used sparingly in jams, drinks, and salads.
Others The mint family is vast; mints cross-pollinate easily and produce variable seedlings, so test a mint for scent and flavour before buying.

MINT, GARDEN
Mentha spicata syn. *Mentha viridis* (Labiatae)
Perennial. see page 61

Origins Native to southern Europe.

Ultimate size 3 × 2ft (90 × 60cm).
Soil Ordinary, damp.
Sun/shade Partial shade.
Description Garden mint is a variable plant with bright green, jagged-edged, spear-shaped leaves. The leaves should have a strong scent of spearmint – fresh and delicious. Purple flowers are borne in whorls up the stems in late summer.
Position As one of the more commonly used culinary herbs, mint needs a bed near a path or the kitchen. A good tip is to remove a paving stone at the edge of a path or patio and plant the mint there – it is then contained, easy to crop, and delicious to smell in passing. It can also be grown in window-boxes or, better still because root growth is then restricted, in an individual pot on a windowsill. In this way fresh mint may be had during the winter months.
Propagation Divide the clumps of roots in the autumn or spring. It is possible to buy mint seed, but as the plants produced will be very variable it is not really to be recommended.
Use The traditional mint to use in mint sauce, jellies, salads and summer drinks.
Others The other main culinary mint is apple mint, which has large, round, hairy leaves with a good strong scent and flavour. Dried peppermint leaves make an excellent tea.

MINT, PINEAPPLE
Mentha rotundifolia 'Variegata' (Labiatae)
Perennial. see page 59

Origins Garden variety of apple mint (*Mentha rotundifolia*).

Ultimate size   3 × 2ft (90 × 60cm).
Soil   Rich, moist.
Sun/shade   Sun or part shade.
Description   A pretty mint with delicate foliage of green splashed with cream; some leaves may be entirely white. Purple flowers in late summer.
Position   Should always be grown with the roots in a container. A very good plant to put in a dull corner, perhaps in front of a bay tree.
Propagation   Split the roots and replant in autumn or spring.
Use   May be used in place of apple mint or garden mint in sauces, soups, or salads or added to peas and potatoes.
Others   Ginger mint (*M. gentilis*) is another very attractive variegated mint – with leaves of gold and green and a spicy scent, it looks very good planted in a border, but the roots are very invasive.

NASTURTIUM, VARIEGATED
Tropaeolum majus 'Alaska' (Tropaeolaceae)
Annual.

Origins   Garden form of a native to Peru.
Ultimate size   1 × 3ft (30 × 90cm).
Soil   Ordinary.
Sun/shade   Sun.
Description   A hardy annual with very attractive leaves of pale green splashed at random with cream. The flowers, in shades of red through orange, start in mid-June and continue all summer – removing the seed pods as they form will encourage the plants to continue flowering.
Position   This nasturtium will trail across the border, so is best toward the front, where the foliage can be seen. It will also grow very successfully in an urn or flower pot, but to ensure plenty of fresh flowers, the plant should be given a liquid feed every week throughout the summer.
Propagation   One of the few variegated plants that will come true when grown from seed. The seed should be sown in early March in a greenhouse – three seeds to a 3in (7.5cm) pot is ideal – or can be sown directly into the border in April.
Use   A versatile plant – the flowers can be stuffed with a cream-cheese mixture and eaten in a salad, or simply scattered on to a salad for added effect. The leaves are peppery and can be shredded and added to salads for extra 'zing', while the unripe seeds can be pickled and used instead of capers in many sauces.
Others   There are a number of different nasturtiums available – dwarf, with flowers of red, orange, or yellow, and climbing plants with various flower colours. Most of the perennial tropaeolums are only half-hardy and are best grown in a cool greenhouse.

ORACH, RED
Atriplex hortensis 'Rubra' (Chenopodiaceae)
Annual.   see page 61

Origins   An ornamental form of a wild plant from central Asia.
Ultimate size   4ft × 1ft 6in (1.4 × 0.45m).
Soil   Moderately rich, well-drained.
Sun/shade   Sun or part shade.
Description   A rather spectacular plant with dark red leaves coming off a tall, red stem. The seeds are covered with a beige, papery skin that looks good in

the early autumn against the red foliage.

Position Thin and tall, the leaves show to their best when planted in large clumps. The sun shining through the leaves gives the effect of a stained-glass window. Red orach looks quite splendid when planted alongside silver plants such as *Artemisia pontica, A. purshiana, A. 'Lambrook Silver'*, and *A. 'Old Warrior'*.

Propagation Orach will self-seed readily if the ripe seeds are allowed to drop in the autumn. Any unwanted seedlings should be hoed out in the spring once they have germinated. Sow in succession to create a continuous effect through the summer.

Use Although they have only a mild flavour, red orach leaves make a colourful and decorative addition to a green salad. Pick while they are still young and tender.

Others The ordinary green orach is an equally tasty salad herb.

ORRIS
Iris germanica (Iridaceae)
Perennial.   see page 68

Origins Southern Europe.
Ultimate size   2ft × 1ft 6in (60 × 45cm).
Soil Neutral, well-drained.
Sun/shade Full sun with the rhizomes just on the surface facing the sun.
Description Glaucous spear-shaped leaves rising in a rosette from the rhizome. The flowers, in late May, are a pale violet.
Position Plant in the sunniest position possible.
Propagation Divide the root stock in late spring

or early autumn. Replant the pieces in their final growing positions.

Use Grown commercially in Tuscany for the production of orris-root powder. The rhizomes are dug up, split, and put to dry for two years before being crushed to a powder. The violet scent becomes stronger, the longer it is allowed to dry.

Others *Iris florentina*, thought to be a sport of *I. germanica*, is the white-flowered iris also grown for its scented rootstock. It has a slightly faded white flower with a tinge of blue and yellow on the beard.

PARSLEY
Petroselinum crispum (Umbelliferae)
Biennial or short-lived perennial.   see page 61

Origins North and central Europe.
Ultimate size   1 × 1ft (30 × 30cm).
Soil Deep, rich, well-dug.
Sun/shade Part shade or full sun.
Description The leaves, at the top of tall, straight stems, are a mass of very curled, dark green leaflets. Flowers, which appear in the second year, should be cut off to encourage fresh leaf growth.
Position Parsley should be grown towards the front of a border where it can be picked with ease. It makes a good border plant.
Propagation Usually grown from seed, but parsley seeds need heat to germinate and then a little patience. Seed should be sown in a seed tray, watered, covered with dark plastic, and put somewhere warm for a week. Remove from the dark and put in a greenhouse (or on a windowsill) at a lower temperature, and within a few days germination

should be well under way. If sowing in the garden, it is best to wait for the soil to warm up in the spring, although some say it helps to pour boiling water in the seed drill first.

Use Parsley has countless uses; it is a must for garnish, used copiously, not in mean little sprigs. It is reputed to counteract the smell of garlic if eaten at the same time. Parsley is supposed to stimulate the appetite – perhaps by enhancing the visual appeal of food.

Others French, Italian, celery-leaf, or plain-leaf parsley – all one and the same plant – is a parsley with large, plain, flat leaves, a strong flavour, and often more vigour than curled parsley. Hamburg parsley (*Petroselinum crispum* 'Tuberosum') is grown for its roots, which are parsnip-like with a flavour between celery and parsley and are used for soups, salads, and vegetable dishes.

Position A pretty spot plant for the front of a border, or a row will make a neat border around a small bed.

Propagation Plants can be grown successfully from seed, but the flowers will be variable in colour. Cuttings may be taken in July and August to increase plants of special varieties.

Use The pink, deliciously fragrant flowers dry well for use in pot-pourris. Shred a few flowers and scatter the petals on to both vegetable and fruit salads.

Others The pink family is very large – clove pinks or border carnations are large-growing and come in a myriad of colours. Maiden pinks (*Dianthus deltoides*) have bright green foliage and flower all summer with small, single flowers of pink and white. They make excellent ground-cover and spot plants, perhaps in paving, but unfortunately have no scent.

PINK, CHEDDAR
Dianthus caesius syn. *D. gratianopolitanus*
(Caryophyllaceae)
Perennial. see page 62

Origins Europe, including Great Britain.
Ultimate size 1 × 1ft (30 × 30cm).
Soil Well-drained, with some well-rotted manure dug in.
Sun/shade Full sun.
Description An excellent plant for a rock garden, with grey-green leaves rising from a tight clump. Fragrant, fringed flowers about 1in (2.5cm) across come in various shades of pink and flower most of the summer.

POKEROOT
Phytolacca americana syn. *P. decandra*
(Phytolaccaceae)
Perennial.

Origin Native to Virginia in the United States, it now grows wild over much of Europe.
Ultimate size 6 × 3ft (2 × 1m).
Soil Ordinary, slightly damp.
Sun/shade Full sun or partial shade.
Description The plant dies back under the soil in the winter and the red buds push through very early in the spring. Fat, hollow, pinkish-green stems rise to pink candelabra flower heads in early summer. By late summer, the flowers have set seeds, which

develop into quite stunning, large, black, maize-like heads. **Warning**: the seeds can be poisonous.

Position A plant that in time will grow to great proportions, it is best planted at the back of a border, where the tempting seed heads will be out of the reach of children.

Propagation The seeds, if allowed to drop in the late autumn, will germinate readily in the spring. The whole plant can be divided if it gets too large.

Use The fruits have been used to help in rheumatic and skin problems and the young shoots have been eaten, but care should be employed – they, too, can be poisonous. It is best grown as an emphatic plant for a large border.

Others *Phytolacca drastica*, which is native to Chile, is an extremely strong purgative.

POPPY 'LADYBIRD'

Papaver commutatum 'Ladybird' (Papaveraceae)
Annual.   see page 62

Origins A garden form of the wild poppy found growing in cornfields and hedgerows in Europe.

Ultimate size 2 × 1ft (60 × 30cm).

Soil Any, if well-drained.

Sun/shade Full sun.

Description A beautiful poppy with dark, glistening-red petals, each with a black spot at the base. Soft, hairy, glaucous leaves.

Position This poppy must be seen, so plant toward the front of a border in a clump of about six plants. As an annual it has a fairly short life, so several successional sowings will be needed to keep a continuous show through the summer.

Propagation Sow the tiny seed in early spring in a seed tray; thin out when large enough and plant out into the garden when about 4in (10cm) tall. Repeat the process about a month later. Save the ripe seed in the autumn for the following year.

Use An invaluable spot plant in the garden. The seeds can be collected when ripe and used to flavour bread and cakes.

Others The poppy family is large and diverse. The soft red petals of the common field poppy have been used to colour medicines. The opium poppy (*Papaver somniferum*), which self-seeds readily in the garden, is much larger, with red, pink, or purple flowers.

PURSLANE

Portulaca oleracea (Portulacaceae)
Annual.

Origins Cultivated for centuries in India and the Middle East.

Ultimate size 6 × 12in (15 × 30cm).

Soil Light, rich, well-drained.

Sun/shade Sun.

Description A creeping plant with small oval leaves, which are thick and very fleshy. The flowers are yellow and come in midsummer.

Position In a sheltered sunny spot in the garden, or may be grown in a pot or trough or even a window-box.

Propagation Grow from seed sown in the spring and thin out the seedlings as soon as they are large enough to handle. Sow successively every month in the summer to ensure a continuous supply.

Use Purslane leaves have a sharp, slightly acid flavour that goes well in salads. The young shoots can be gently cooked and eaten as a vegetable.

Others *Portulaca oleracea* 'Sativa' is an attractive golden-leaved variety.

QUEEN OF THE MEADOW

Eupatorium purpureum (Compositae)
Perennial.   see page 46

Origins North America.
Ultimate size 6 × 3ft (2 × 1m).
Soil Rich, limey, dry or moist.
Sun/shade Sun or partial shade.
Description Slender, pointed, mid-green leaves grow in whorls up the stems, which are topped by fluffy heads of pink florets. Bumblebees and butterflies find the florets addictive – they sit on them in soporific trances for hours. The stems are strong enough not to need staking.
Position Particularly good for the back of a border, Queen of the meadow does very well in partnership with teasels.
Propagation Cut down to ground level in late autumn. Divide and replant between October and March.
Use A decoction from the root has been used in the treatment of renal disorders.
Others A large genus of variable plants. *Eupatorium purpureum roseum* has very dark red florets and stalks; hemp agrimony (*E. cannabinum*), which can be found growing wild alongside streams and rivers, has attractive soft pink flowers and cannabis-like leaves.

ROCKET

Eruca sativa (Cruciferae)
Annual.

Origins Native to southern Europe.
Ultimate size 18 × 6in (45 × 15cm).
Soil Good, well-drained.
Sun/Shade Sun.
Description A tall, thin plant with small, mid-green leaves borne on a single stem that is topped by pretty, cream-coloured flowers during the summer months.
Position Grow in a border whose soil has been enriched or it can be grown in a decorative pot or trough.
Propagation Rocket seed should be sown in early spring, and the seedlings pricked out when large enough to handle and planted out in their final position when about 3in (7.5cm) high. Use the leaves when they are still young – if they are not picked frequently the plant will quickly run to flower. However, if the flowering stem is pinched out good growth is encouraged. Sow successively throughout the summer to ensure a good supply of fresh leaves.
Use With their slightly peppery flavour, rocket leaves are delicious when shredded into salads – a mixture of purslane, rocket, and sorrel leaves shredded into a green salad makes a world of difference to it. It is a good addition to a tomato and onion salad. The leaves can also be used as a vegetable.
Others As a salad herb, rocket belongs in the group also containing purslane, dandelion, and fennel.

ROSA MUNDI
Rosa gallica 'Versicolor' (Rosaceae)
Shrub.   see page 64

Origins A natural sport of *Rosa gallica* 'Officinalis'.
Ultimate size 3 × 3ft (1 × 1m).
Soil Deep, rich loam enriched with well-rotted manure.
Sun/shade Full sun.
Description One of the most striking of the *gallicas*, the flowers are semi-double, light red, striped with white and pink, but each is different. The plant has good green foliage, which provides a superb background for the flowers, few thorns, and a fine perfume.
Position As for the eglantine rose. The Rosa Mundi is excellent for hedging, but is also good in a formal herb garden.
Propagation Propagation is best left to the experts, but it is possible to take cuttings in the summer.
Use Most useful as a garden shrub in its own right, although the flowers can be used in cooking in the same way as those of *R. gallica* 'Officinalis' (see below).
Others Other *gallicas* include 'Tuscany Superb', which has large double flowers of a dark maroon-crimson. 'Hippolyte' is a soft violet double, with a button eye and arching branches. 'Duchesse d'Angoulême' is a good rose for a smaller garden, keeping a compact shape. The flowers are very fragrant, fully double, pale pink, sometimes with a crimson edge.

ROSE, APOTHECARY'S
Rosa gallica 'Officinalis' (Rosaceae)
Shrub.

Origins The apothecary's rose was well known during the heyday of the Roman Empire and is known to have been cultivated in France in the 12th and 13th centuries. It is thought that the original rose came from Asia Minor, before being distributed all over the world.
Ultimate size 3 × 3ft (1 × 1m).
Soil Deep, rich loam, enriched with well-rotted manure.
Sun/shade Sunny beds and borders.
Description A late-flowering, strongly perfumed rose with light red, semi-double flowers and bright yellow stamens. The bright green foliage is abundant, with few thorns. Small, red fruits follow in the autumn.
Position A lovely shrub rose for any border, it looks and smells wonderful when planted in conjunction with a semi-evergreen honeysuckle, *Lonicera japonica* 'Halliana'.
Propagation Propagating roses is really a job for the experts. It is quite possible, however, to take cuttings of favourite roses and grow them on their own roots. If growing from seeds, the plants produced may be very different from their parents.
Use The apothecary's rose was originally grown for a variety of purposes – to make conserves, syrups, rosewater, creams, and ointments. The flowers dry well and, if picked in bud, will make an excellent addition to a pot-pourri. Use the petals in salads and rosewater to flavour drinks.

Others The *gallica* family of roses is a large one containing several well-known varieties – 'Cardinal de Richelieu' has dark, velvety purple flowers; 'Charles de Mills' has large double maroon flowers which fade to grey; 'Complicata' has fairly large, single, pink flowers and makes a large, rampant plant; 'Tricolore de Flandre' has fully double flowers of magenta-purple striped with rose-pink and mauve.

ROSE, EGLANTINE
Rosa eglantaria, syn. *R. rubiginosa* (Rosaceae)
Rambler.   see page 64

Origins Europe, including Great Britain.
Ultimate Size 7 × 5ft (2 × 1.5m).
Soil Rich, well-drained.
Sun/shade Sun, partial shade.
Description The eglantine rose is marked by the amazing scent of its leaves, which, particularly in damp weather, is of apples. The flowers are single, pink with yellow stamens. Red hips are borne in abundance in the autumn. Very vicious thorns are usually a trade mark of this rose, which makes it an excellent plant for a hedge.
Position Plant well away from paths, as the branches can grow up to 6ft (2m) a year, but plant somewhere where the wonderful scent can waft around on a damp day. Good for hedging, it will also make a screen against a fence. Cut back fairly hard each autumn or spring to keep the growth under control.
Propagation If the hips are allowed to drop and lie in the border, they will probably produce a few

seedlings the following summer. Take cuttings of non-flowering shoots in August, dip them into rooting hormone, place in a sheltered bed, and leave until the following year before planting out into the final bed.
Use The petals can be used to make jams and conserves, while the hips can be made into rose-hip syrup and teas.
Others Also known as Penzance briers, after Lord Penzance who raised them, the hybrid sweet briers are attractive in flower and are richly scented – 'Lady Penzance' has single flowers with rich, coppery tints, 'Amy Robsart' is rich, rose-pink with semi-double flowers, 'Lord Penzance' has buff flowers, flushed pink, while 'Meg Merrilees' has bright crimson, double flowers with an exceptionally strong scent.

ROSEMARY
Rosmarinus officinalis (Labiatae)
Evergreen perennial.   see page 66

Origins Native to the Mediterranean coast.
Ultimate size 3ft × 1ft 6in (90 × 45cm).
Soil Well-drained.
Sun/shade Full sun.
Description An aromatic, evergreen perennial with short, spiky leaves of a glaucous green. The pale blue flowers appear on the young growth in early spring.
Position Rosemaries should be grown in sheltered corners, protected from cold winter winds. They make excellent hedges, and should be clipped a couple of times a year, in late spring and late summer. It is worth growing a hedge of mixed

lavender and rosemary, which gives two wonderful scents and two different flowering periods. Rosemaries grow well tucked against a house, at the edge of steps or on a wall, where they benefit from the good drainage and can be brushed in passing to release their heavenly scent.

Propagation Best grown from cuttings, taken in midsummer when the wood has begun to harden a little, they usually root readily in a sandy soil in a cold frame. Plant out the following year.

Use Rosemary has many uses, most commonly as a flavouring of meats – especially lamb and chicken. The oil may be used as an insect repellant and is also widely used in the cosmetic industry, particularly in shampoos. Spread a few twigs on the fire when cooking on a barbeque – the scent will make all the difference.

Others There are some quite lovely varieties of rosemary – some with pink flowers, some white, and some very deep blue. Prostrate rosemary grows almost flat, but is slightly frost-tender. The variety 'Benenden Blue' has very fine, strongly aromatic foliage with dark blue flowers; 'Miss Jessopp's Upright' grows tall and columnar; and 'Majorca', with spiky foliage and pink flowers, has a tendency to trail.

RUE 'JACKMAN'S BLUE'

Ruta graveolens 'Jackman's Blue' (Rutaceae)
Perennial. see page 59

Origins Southern Europe.
Ultimate size 2ft × 1ft 6in (60 × 45cm).
Soil Ordinary, well-drained.

Sun/shade Full sun.
Description A neat shrub whose finely divided blue-green foliage has a strong, slightly acrid scent. Waxy, yellow flowers follow in summer. To keep the plant a tidy shape, and to prevent the flowers from coming too early in the year and so spoiling the colour and shape of the plant, cut back hard to about 1ft (30cm) from the ground in mid-April, after the heaviest frosts are over.

Position With its lovely blue foliage, rue should be seen toward the front of a border. It blends well with silver plants, looking splendid when planted in large swathes.

Propagation Seeds can be sown in early spring, but bought seeds will often produce a plant with inferior-coloured foliage. It is best to take cuttings from the ripe wood in August, in a sand and peat mix, overwinter in a cold frame, and plant out the following year. **Warning:** gloves should be worn, as many people suffer from allergic reactions to rue.

Use The prime use has to be as a spot plant for a border. The leaves have been used medicinally in the past, and they can be shredded very sparingly into a salad. As the scent is so very strong, the flavour is also strong – and an acquired taste.

Others The ordinary rue, usually grown from seed, has slightly washed-out blue foliage. Variegated rue has blue foliage splashed liberally with cream.

SAGE

Salvia officinalis (Labiatae)
Evergreen, perennial shrub. see page 68

Origins Southern Europe.

Ultimate size 2 × 1ft (60 × 30cm).
Soil Well-drained, light.
Sun/shade Full sun.
Description A hardy, evergreen shrub with large, soft, downy leaves of a grey-green colour that have a strong scent. The flowers may be of blue, pink, or white, but, unless the plant is being grown as a garden plant to show off the flowers, it is best to pinch out the flower buds as they form, to encourage fresh leaf growth and to keep the plant a tidy shape. Sage should not be allowed to grow too tall and leggy – it will not take having the old wood cut into so should be pinched out little and often through the growing season.
Position Sage is a good plant to plant toward the front of a bed – it can be easily reached to pick the leaves for cooking, and the scent wafts up when brushed in passing.
Propagation Sage can be grown from seed, but the resulting plants have a tendency to go quickly to flower and so lose their shape. It is best to grow sage from cuttings, taken from ripe wood in September, rooted in a peat and sand mix in a cold frame, and plant out the plants the following spring. Pinch out the growing tips as soon as the plant starts to grow. A plant that has become too leggy may be stem-rooted, by pinning a branch to the soil, where it will root *in situ*. The rooted branch can then be severed and planted elsewhere or can replace the parent plant.
Use Traditionally used for stuffing poultry and meats. It is a vital ingredient in many herb cheeses and pickles. Sage tea is used to purify the blood.
Others The salvia family is very large – many of the more ornamental varieties are frost-tender. The broad-leaf sage, which is perhaps the best form to grow for culinary use, seldom flowers, while the Spanish sage (*Salvia hispanica*) has smaller, grey leaves and produces attractive dark blue flowers in early summer. *S. triloba*, found in southern Europe, has hairy grey-green foliage with a strong flavour and pale blue flowers – it is an interesting alternative to common sage, but does best when kept frost-free.

SAGE, PINEAPPLE
Salvia rutilans (Labiatae)
Perennial.   see page 68

Origins South America.
Ultimate size 3ft × 1ft 6in (90 × 45cm).
Soil Well-drained.
Sun/shade Full sun.
Description A fascinating plant with quite large, pale green leaves that have a strong scent of pineapples when bruised. The flowers of bright scarlet appear in late summer, reaching their peak by Christmas.
Position It will grow quite large if planted out in the border. However, because it is frost-tender, it may be best to grow pineapple sage in a flower pot, to keep it small and to bring the pot into a frost-free environment at the start of cold weather. The pot can be stood on a patio all summer, where the plant will release its scent when brushed in passing.
Propagation Pineapple sage roots very easily from cuttings taken at any time of the year.
Use The pineapple flavour is very faint, but adds an interesting extra taste if a few leaves are placed in the baking tin before adding the batter when making a plain sponge cake. A few leaves could also be chopped and sprinkled into a fruit salad.

Others The very similar but smaller *Salvia elegans* has smaller leaves and scarlet flowers all summer with a more fruity scent to the leaves. Of the other salvias, most have scented foliage – *S. neurepia* has blackcurrant-scented leaves. *S. patens* needs to be treated like a dahlia, its rhizomes lifted and kept dry and frost free in the winter. It has wonderful, dark, sky-blue flowers in late summer.

SAGE, PURPLE
Salvia officinalis 'Purpurascens' (Labiatae)
Evergreen perennial. see page 66

Origins Garden form of *Salvia officinalis* (see above).
Ultimate size 1ft 6in × 1ft (45 × 30cm).
Soil Well-drained, light.
Sun/shade Full sun.
Description A very attractive plant with purple-red leaves often randomly streaked with green or cream. Purple sage produces spikes of dark blue flowers in midsummer, which should be pinched off as soon as they finish to keep the plant a good shape.
Position With the spectacular colour of the foliage, purple sage must be planted where it can be seen – as a large block in a corner of a border or even, in a formal many-bedded garden, a whole bed.
Propagation Purple sage can be propagated domestically only from cuttings taken in the early autumn and planted out the following spring. It is possible to propagate sages by micropropagation (growing new plants, identical to the parent plant, from cell culture), but this is not really something for the amateur to attempt.

Use Although it is perfectly in order to eat the coloured-leaf sages, the prime use for purple sage is to make a tea from the leaves – it is reputed to be soothing for sore throats.
Others *Salvia icterina* has gold-green variegated foliage. It is very attractive though slightly less easy to grow and, again, is best when planted in a large mass. Tricolour sage (*S. tricolor*) has leaves of green, pink, and cream all splashed at random. It makes a lovely spot plant, but does not appreciate damp soils and atmosphere, so tends to be short lived.

SALVIA GLUTINOSA
(Labiatae)
Perennial.

Origins Europe.
Ultimate Size 3ft × 1ft 6in (90 × 45cm).
Soil Any garden soil.
Sun/shade Sun or partial shade.
Description A large herbaceous plant with pale green, aromatic, slightly sticky foliage. The flowers, coming in late summer, are unusual for a salvia, being a soft yellow.
Position Being fairly tall growing, it is best placed at the back of a shallow border, perhaps behind some pinks or marjorams, and in front of an angelica or climbing rose.
Propagation The clumps can be split and replanted in the spring or autumn. Seed can be collected and sown in the spring, and the young plants planted out in the autumn.
Use The seeds yield an aromatic gum.
Others *Salvia sclarea*, clary sage, is a biennial with

large silver-green leaves that make a spectacular display in midsummer. *S. argentea* is a short-lived perennial with rosettes of silky, silver leaves and white flowers in midsummer.

SANTOLINA, GREEN
Santolina viridis syn. *Santolina virens* (Compositae)
Evergreen, perennial shrub.

Origins Southern Europe, north Africa.
Ultimate size 1ft 6in × 1ft 6in (45 × 45cm).
Soil Light, well-drained.
Sun/shade Full sun.
Description A green-leaved santolina, whose flowers look wonderful when allowed to develop into a dark yellow cloud over dark green bushes. Clipped into a round shape in the spring, *Santolina viridis* makes a neat focal point in a garden and blends well with other softer shapes and foliages.
Position *S. viridis* makes a very good specimen plant in a herb garden. Growing smaller than the common santolina, it looks good on the edge of a patio or in a dwarf bed.
Propagation Cuttings of semi-ripe wood should be taken in midsummer, before flowering. Root in a peat and sand mix and plant the rooted cuttings into their final positions the following autumn or spring.
Use The slightly scented foliage is good in flower arrangements and, dried, in pot-pourri. Branches, laid in drawers, are said to deter moths.
Others Other green-leaved santolinas include *S. pinnata*, with soft-cream flowers, and 'Lemon Queen', which has soft green foliage and pale cream flowers.

SAVORY, CREEPING
Satureja repandra (Labiatae)
Semi-evergreen perennial.   see page 68

Origins Europe.
Ultimate size 2 × 12in (5 × 30cm).
Soil Well-drained.
Sun/shade Full sun.
Description A very pretty savory, with bright green, spiky leaves on short branches that trail over the ground. The branches are covered with a mass of white flowers in late summer. The plant will often appear to die completely in the winter, but should grow again when the weather warms up.
Position The front of the border is the obvious place to site creeping savory, though it will be very happy on the edge of a patio.
Propagation Cuttings, taken in the early summer, root readily and should be planted out the following spring.
Use If winter savory is not available, snip a few creeping-savory leaves in to a home-made cream-cheese mix, together with lots of parsley.
Others Purple-flowered savory (*Satureja montana coerulea*) bears pretty flowers in late summer.

SAVORY, SUMMER
Satureja hortensis (Labiatae)
Annual.

Origins Native to eastern Mediterranean regions and Asia.

Ultimate size   12 × 6in (30 × 15cm).
Soil   Ordinary, well-drained.
Sun/shade   Full sun.
Description   A tender, strongly aromatic plant with dark green, spiky, scented leaves and tiny pink flowers in late summer.
Position   In a sunny border or as a hedging plant.
Propagation   Grow from seed, but do not sow too early in the year because summer savory is liable to damp off in cool, dull weather. Plants left to themselves in the autumn will often self-seed in the following year.
Use   In parts of Europe summer savory is known as the bean herb, because it is delicious when cooked with pulses, especially, perhaps, broad beans. If you wish to dry it for winter use, cut it just before flowering, dry it, and store it in a dark glass jar.
Others   Winter savory (see next entry) has a slightly coarser taste.

SAVORY, WINTER
Satureja montana (Labiatae)
Evergreen perennial.   see page 71

Origins   Europe, Asia.
Ultimate size   1 × 1ft (30 × 30cm).
Soil   Well-drained.
Sun/shade   Full sun.
Description   A small, bushy, compact shrub with spiky, green leaves with a strong, aromatic scent. Tiny, white-pink flowers are borne in the leaf axils in late summer. The plant will get very woody within a few years and is best replaced every three years or so.
Position   A small plant that should be sited at the front of a border, or can make a small, informal hedge. The dead flower stalks should be trimmed off to tidy the plant at the end of the autumn, with a full clip back to about 8in (20cm) in the spring.
Propagation   Although it is possible to grow winter savory from seed, the plants will be slow to establish and very variable in habit. It is best to take cuttings of semi-ripe wood in May, keeping the rooted plants in a cold frame, to plant out the following year.
Use   Savory has a strong, spicy flavour and goes very well with cheese and breads. It is good to add to soups and stews.
Others   Summer savory (see previous entry) is an annual with a less strong flavour. It goes especially well with beans, both fresh and dried.

SORREL
Rumex scutatus (Polygonaceae)
Perennial.   see page 71

Origins   Europe and Asia.
Ultimate size   1 × 1ft (30 × 30cm).
Soil   Ordinary, moist.
Sun/shade   Sun or partial shade.
Description   Sorrel's bright green leaves, coming from a central crown, have a strongly acidic flavour. Sometimes the plant will throw up a tall flower spike, which is very unexciting, with small brown flowers. It should be removed immediately to encourage the growth of the valuable, lush leaves.
Position   Not an especially attractive plant, so it may be better to relegate it to a corner out of sight.
Propagation   As this form of sorrel seldom

flowers, and should be discouraged from doing so, it can really only be multiplied by division. It is best to have several plants growing in a large group, and lift and divide the plants every other year. They grow quite fast, but continual cropping of a single plant will weaken it.

Use The tastily acidic leaves are wonderful when finely shredded and added to a green salad – about two leaves to one lettuce. Sorrel soup, making use of overblown lettuce and a few sorrel leaves, is a delicious summer appetizer.

Others The common sorrel is very similar in appearance, but has coarser leaves and runs quickly to seed. The flavour is the same. Buckler-leaved sorrel, *Rumex acetosa*, has small, shield-shaped leaves which, though quite attractive, take rather a long time to harvest. *R. obtusifolius* is the common dock that in Britain is applied to relieve a nettle sting.

SOUTHERNWOOD
Artemisia abrotanum (Compositae)
Shrub.   see page 59

Origins Southern Europe.
Ultimate size 3 × 3ft (1 × 1m).
Soil Light, well-drained.
Sun/shade Full sun.
Description A hardy, bushy, erect shrub with soft, fine foliage in summer that has a wonderful lemony scent. The leaves die off in the winter and the plant does look rather untidy for a while, but growth starts early in the spring. Once the worst of the frosts are over, cut the plant hard back to maintain a good shape, otherwise it will get very tall and straggly. The fresh green growth will spring out from low down the stems, and it will quickly become an aromatic green ball. The rather dreary, yellow flowers are borne in late summer.

Position Valuable as a single shrub, southernwood also looks wonderful planted in a large mass of several plants together. The finely cut foliage teams up well with lavender 'Hidcote' and *Artemisia absinthium* 'Lambrook Silver'. Several planted in a row will make a very effective hedge, needing clipping only twice a year, in late spring and late summer.

Propagation Root cuttings of semi-ripe wood in August in sandy soil. Overwinter in a cold frame and plant out the following spring as required in the garden.

Use The old English name for southernwood, 'Garde robe', suggests that branches were hung in cupboards to keep moths away; sprigs were also spread on floors to keep the atmosphere sweet in houses with little sanitation or fresh air. Today it is seldom used, but it is an excellent herb for flower arrangers because of the beautiful decorative leaves and its delicate fragrance.

Others The artemisia family is quite large, made up of herbaceous, hardy, half-hardy, evergreen, and deciduous plants. Wormwood, (*A. absinthium*) is a hardy shrub with green-silver leaves and a strong scent. *A. caucasica* (syn. *A. pedemontana* and *A. lanata*) is a very dwarf creeping plant with finely cut silver foliage. Almost all the artemisias have dreary, groundsel-like flowers – they are seldom produced in cold regions – that add little to the charm of the foliage of this plant; they should be pinched out as they develop.

STRAWBERRY, ALPINE
Fragaria vesca (Rosaceae)
Semi-evergreen perennial.

Origins Europe and North America.
Ultimate size 12 × 6in (30 × 15cm).
Soil Rich.
Sun/shade Sun or partial shade.
Description Small, bright green plants with heavily veined foliage. The tiny, white flowers appear prolifically in early summer and carry on until the first frosts of autumn. Alpine strawberries do not usually send out runners and will seed themselves lavishly if not picked bare.
Position A pretty plant to put at the front of a border, or to make a small hedge around a bed. It is a good idea to place the plants where children will not cause too much damage when foraging for the delicious fruit.
Propagation The plants can be split, but will usually self-seed in the bed quite readily. Seed can be bought, but is quite slow to germinate. It takes about four months to grow a fruiting plant from seed.
Use There is surely no need to describe the pleasures of eating fresh strawberries, no matter how tiny. It takes quite a few plants to produce reasonable quantities of fruit, but a few for garnish, or to keep children happy in the garden after a leisurely Sunday lunch, are still a joy. An infusion of the leaves is an astringent.
Others The common, wild strawberry is very similar, producing slightly smaller fruit. A yellow-fruiting variety has been introduced, but yellow strawberries don't seem to have quite the same appeal.

SWEET CICELY
Myrrhis odorata (Umbelliferae)
Perennial. see page 72

Origins Northern Europe, including Great Britain.
Ultimate Size 3ft × 1ft 6in (90 × 45cm).
Soil Good, moist.
Sun/shade Sun or part shade.
Description Fragrant, fern-like leaves with a hint of aniseed. Flat white flower heads, like cow parsley, cover the plant in spring, followed by large, green seeds, about 1in (2.5cm) long, which turn jet black by the time they are ripe. The plant will die down completely in late autumn, but is one of the first to reappear in the spring.
Position An invaluable plant to put in a partially shaded bed, it will also flourish in full sun. Being quite tall, it is best behind some of the smaller plants – it grows very prettily in partnership with comfrey (*Symphytum officinale*) and woodruff (*Asperula odorata*).
Propagation It is best to allow a few seeds to drop in the border and let them self-seed. If sown artificially, the seed should be sown in a seed tray, covered with compost, and left outside for several months – it must have several hard frosts with some periods above freezing in between. As soon as the weather warms up the seeds should germinate easily.
Use A valuable culinary herb, all parts of the plant can be eaten – the leaves are slightly sweet and can be

added to stewed fruit to reduce the amount of sugar needed. The seeds, when ripe, can be crushed and added to a sweet-crumble mix or to a fruit pudding. The roots may be washed, boiled, and eaten as a vegetable, or allowed to cool, dressed with a salad dressing, and eaten as a salad.

Others Many other plants look very similar to sweet cicely, but few are edible, so beware that what is being eaten is the true plant.

SWEET ROCKET
Hesperis matronalis (Cruciferae)
Biennial or short-lived perennial.   see page 63

Origins Southern Europe.
Ultimate size   3ft × 1ft (90 × 30cm).
Soil Rich, moist.
Sun/shade Sun/partial shade.
Description Clumps of dark green leaves out of which rise spikes abundantly covered with cross-shaped flowers of pure white. The scent of the flowers is most noticeable at dusk. Cutting off the flowering spikes after flowering will prolong the life of the plant by discouraging it from setting seed.
Position A wonderful plant for an herbaceous border, it looks quite spectacular when planted next to a clump of 'Forcaste' chives and green fennel. Plant a clump near a patio or under a window that is often open in the summer so that you can appreciate the evening scent.
Propagation It is easy to buy seed of sweet rocket from a reputable seed merchant. If you have a particularly good specimen in the garden, allow it to set seed and collect the seed when the pod is brown

and dry and just beginning to open. If other sweet rockets with different flower colours are growing nearby, the seeds may not produce flowers with the identical colour.
Use A wonderful spot plant for the border, with the added advantage of sweet scent in the evening. The seeds were reputed to be a cure for bites and stings, and were sometimes mixed with vinegar to cure freckles.
Others Purple-flowered sweet rocket is common. Double-flowered forms are rare, but can be found. There is a dwarf form, 'Candidissima', which grows to about 15in (45cm).

TARRAGON, FRENCH
Artemisia dracunculus (Compositae)
Perennial.

Origins Southern Europe.
Ultimate size   18in × 12in (50cm × 30cm).
Soil Warm, well-drained, light. In areas with cold, wet, and heavy soil, it is a good idea to grow tarragon in a container – this will enable you to provide a well-drained medium for strong root growth, and the whole pot could be placed in a dry, sheltered place in the winter for extra protection.
Sun/shade Full sun.
Description A rather unassuming plant that gives a quite special flavour. The leaves are pale green, slightly hairy, narrow and about 1in (2cm) long. Several stalks will rise from an underground cluster of roots, which will produce an abundance of leaves if kept from flowering. The flowers, coming at the end of the summer, are very dull, small, green buds

that seldom open and almost never set seed. They are usually sterile.

Position Having no great ornamental value, tarragon merits no special position in the garden. Best confined to the culinary herb garden or to a container.

Propagation French tarragon is sterile, so cannot be grown from seed. Plants may be split in the spring or autumn, or cuttings may be taken in early summer, though to root cuttings is a rather chancy business. Commercially, most French tarragon is now grown by tissue culture, growing new plants from individual cells under laboratory conditions.

Use Tarragon is slightly aniseed flavoured and people tend to like or loathe it. It is a vital ingredient in a *fines herbes* mix – 1 part tarragon, 1 part chervil, 1 part chives, and 2 parts parsley. It goes especially well when used in partnership with egg and chicken dishes. Being herbaceous, it will die down in the winter; to preserve tarragon for winter use, try chopping a good handful, mixing it with a good French mustard, and keeping it in a sealed jar. This tarragon mustard is excellent cooked with chicken breasts or served with cold meats. Tarragon is one of the few herbs we have found that dries well in a microwave oven. Spread a handful of leaves on some kitchen paper, cover with more paper, and dry on 'hot' for about 30 seconds. Check to see if the leaves have dried, and if not give a little longer. Check frequently to ensure that the leaves do not burn. When quite dry, cool and bottle in a dark jar, and use through the winter until the new fresh crop starts to grow enough to pick in the spring.

Others There is no substitute for true French tarragon. Russian tarragon (*Artemisia dracunculoides*) grows very much taller and with more vigour, but to most discerning palates bears no comparison. It will grow from seed, so always beware if buying so called 'French tarragon' seed.

TEASEL
Dipsacus fullonum (Dipsacaceae)
Perennial. see page 72

Origins Europe and North America.
Ultimate size 3–6ft × 1ft 6in (1–2 × 0.5m).
Soil Damp.
Sun/shade Sun or part shade.
Description Easily recognized by the blunt, conical flower heads, which stay on the dead stalks all winter. The bright green, prickly leaves and stem join together to form a 'cup' that will hold water for insects to drink from. Tiny, purple flowers open in rings around the flower head in summer, then die off to leave the typical teasel.
Position A tall, stately plant, the teasel is best sited at the back of a border where it can tower over the smaller plants when in flower. The large leaves of the juvenile plant look good near chives, fennels, and burdocks, giving a wonderful colour and shape contrast.
Propagation Teasels will self-seed happily wherever they grow, readily producing vast quantities of seeds. The seed germinates quickly and easily, but it is seldom necessary to germinate artificially as the beds will usually have plenty of seedlings coming up in the spring.
Use Traditionally, the flower heads were collected in the autumn, when quite dry and dead, and used to card wool. Today they are seldom used in the

woollen industry, but they make stunning additions to flower arrangements in the garden and in the house. According to Culpeper, the roots have a cleansing faculty.

Others Other thistle-like plants have equally stately growth, but they do not always make such useful plants for the florist – the Scotch thistle (*Onopordon acanthium*) is an enormous plant with sharply cut silver foliage and typical thistle heads; the holy thistle, *Cnicus benedictus*, is low-growing with soft, hairy foliage and small, unexciting flowers.

THYME
Thymus vulgaris (Labiatae)
Evergreen, perennial shrub.   see page 75

Origins Southern Europe.
Ultimate size 1 × 1ft (30 × 30cm).
Soil Light, rich.
Sun/shade Full sun.
Description A small shrub with dark green, aromatic, narrow leaves. Small, pink flowers appear from the leaf axils in June–July. Thyme does not take happily to being cut back too hard, so should be kept trimmed frequently to keep a neat shape and to prevent the growth from getting straggly.
Position Thyme is best grown towards the front of the border, where it can be picked easily when needed. It likes some protection from cold winter winds. In a sheltered garden it will make an attractive low hedge. It does not in the least object to constant clipping.
Propagation Although it is possible to grow thyme from seed, better plants will often be produced from small cuttings taken in early summer and struck in sandy soil, to plant out in late summer. A plant that has become woody and straggly could have a branch pegged down on to the ground, where it will root. Sever the rooted branch the following spring and plant it to replace the old parent.

Use One of the traditional herbs to mix into a stuffing for meats or vegetables, thyme has a fairly strong flavour and should be used in moderation. The leaves are antiseptic and make a healing gargle for sore throats.

Others There are several varieties of thyme – lemon thyme (*Thymus citriodorus*) is very similar in appearance, but the leaves have a strong lemon scent. 'Silver Queen' and 'Golden King' are lemon thymes with variegated foliage. 'Lemon Curd' is particularly sweet-scented.

THYME, CRIMSON
Thymus serpyllum 'Coccineus' (Labiatae)
Evergreen, creeping shrublet.

Origins Garden form of *Thymus serpyllum*, which grows wild in much of Europe.
Ultimate size 3 × 12in (7.5 × 30cm).
Soil Light, rich.
Sun/shade Full sun.
Description A beautiful variety of creeping thyme with small, dark green leaves and rich, crimson flowers in midsummer.
Position A must to plant in a crack in paving on a patio, or to plant in a pocket in a terracotta herb pot.
Use Too small to be of much herbal use, it is best

appreciated for the wonderful colour of the flowers.

Others Several creeping thymes have interesting flower colours – 'Annie Hall' has pale green foliage with pink flowers, 'Snowdrift' has pure white flowers, and 'Pink Chintz' has pale pink flowers.

THYME 'DOONE VALLEY'

Thymus 'Doone Valley' (Labiatae)
Evergreen, creeping shrublet.   see page 75

Origins Garden form.
Ultimate size 6 × 12in (15 × 30cm).
Soil Light, rich.
Sun/shade Full sun.
Description A creeping thyme with green leaves, heavily splashed with gold; small, pink flowers are borne in midsummer. The foliage has a strong, lemon scent.
Position An attractive thyme to plant in a crack in paving, at the edge of a path, or at the front of a border. If the site is not sunny, the leaves have a tendency to lose their variegation.
Propagation This thyme can only be grown from cuttings, but it will root very easily. A small piece, pinned on to the ground, will root *in situ* within two to three weeks, and can then be dug up and replanted where required.
Use It is more a decorative plant than a culinary herb, but there is no reason why a few sprigs should not be used in cooking if space is too limited to grow a special culinary variety.
Others Other creeping, lemon-scented thymes include 'Creeping Lemon', with dark green foliage and bright pink flowers in midsummer and 'Wild

Lemon', with small, green leaves and a strong, lemon scent. *Thymus herba barona* has caraway-scented foliage, *T. mastochinus* has leaves that smell of lavender, and *T. fragrantissimus* has leaves with a strong hint of orange.

THYME 'SILVER POSIE'

Thymus vulgaris (Labiatae)
Evergreen shrub.

Origins Garden variety.
Ultimate size 1 × 1ft (30 × 30cm).
Soil Light, rich, garden soil.
Sun/shade Full sun.
Description A very attractive, upright-growing thyme with silver-variegated foliage and pale pink flowers in summer. If the occasional branch loses its variegation be sure to cut it out quickly before the green growth takes over and the plant loses its silver variegation.
Propagation This thyme is easily propagated from cuttings, either by rooting a small piece in the ground alongside the parent plant or striking a few cuttings during the early summer into a sandy soil mix.
Position A good plant to fill in a small patch between other, dark-leaved, herbs – bugle (*Ajuga reptans*) or broad-leaf thyme, for example. It will also make a pretty, dwarf hedge to border a small bed.
Use Use in cooking as you would common thyme.
Others Other upright thymes include *T. vulgaris* 'Aureus', with small, gold leaves and tiny, pink flowers. *T. nitidus* makes a neat bush of tiny, green

leaves and white flowers while *T. erectus* grows in tall, thin spikes with white flowers.

VALERIAN
Valeriana officinalis (Valerianaceae)
Perennial.   see pages 61 and 76

Origins Northern Europe.
Ultimate size 6ft × 1ft 6in (2 × 0.5m).
Soil Ordinary.
Sun/shade Sun.
Description The first shoots in spring are reddish-purple, rising to tall spikes of pale green, topped with umbel-like clusters of pale pink flowers in midsummer.
Position A lovely plant for the edge of a border, especially when planted in association with honeysuckles – in particular, *Lonicera × americana*. It needs to be cut down as soon as the flowering period is over, as it then has a tendency to look very scruffy and untidy, and the seeds will spread everywhere.
Propagation Escaped seedlings can be dug up in the spring and replanted where required. Ripe seed can be collected and sown in the spring in a seed tray in a greenhouse.
Use A medicinal herb whose roots are used to make a soothing tea. The leaves are attractive to cats, who like to nibble at the young growth in spring. The roots may be used to flavour soups.
Others An attractive form of valerian that does not grow to such heights is *Valerian phu* 'Aurea', with golden-yellow shoots and tiny, white flowers in late summer.

VIOLET
Viola odorata (Violaceae)
Perennial.   see page 77

Origins Europe.
Ultimate size 6 × 12in (15 × 30cm).
Soil Ordinary, enriched with well-rotted manure.
Sun/shade Part sun, shade.
Description Heart-shaped leaves of mid-green form a tight mound from which the violet or white flowers arise. The flowers are sweetly scented, usually showing from February to April, and often again in the autumn.
Position An enchanting plant for the front of a border or along the edge of a path, where the pretty flowers can be easily seen.
Propagation The whole plant can be split in the late summer, or cuttings can be taken of non-flowering shoots in July, planting them out in the late autumn or spring. The plants will usually self-seed readily, and seedlings can be dug up and replanted in late spring.
Use Violet flowers can be candied for cake decorating, and with their slightly spicy flavour they also make an unusual and colourful addition to a green salad. The leaves have been used in herbal medicines as a tonic and to heal wounds.
Others There are several named varieties of violets – 'Christmas', an early-flowering form, has white flowers with a green eye; 'Czar' has deep purple flowers, 'Sulphurea' has apricot-yellow flowers which are flushed with violet-purple when they are in bud; 'Marie Louise' is a double mauve form.

VIPER'S BUGLOSS
Echium vulgare (Boraginaceae)
Biennial. see page 78

Origins England.
Ultimate size 2 × 1ft (60 × 30cm).
Soil Ordinary, well-drained.
Sun/shade Sun.
Description A very hairy biennial that, in the first year, makes a large rosette of narrow leaves. In the second year a profusion of bright blue flowers is carried on short spikes. They bloom from June to August and are very attractive to bees.
Position With the beautiful, blue flowers, bugloss could be grown anywhere in the garden, but it looks especially good when planted near bergamots and mallows.
Propagation If the plants are allowed to die *in situ*, the seeds will drop around the parent plants and germinate readily the following spring.
Use Bugloss has been used medicinally to alleviate headaches and fevers.
Others There are several other echiums. Some are half-hardy and grow in the Mediterranean regions; others, such as *Echium plantagineum*, are grown as bedding plants for summer display.

WINTERGREEN
Gaultheria procumbens (Ericaceae)
Evergreen perennial. see page 79

Origins Northeastern America.

Ultimate size 6in × 3ft (15cm × 1m).
Soil Moist, acid, with added peat or lime-free leaf mould.
Sun/shade Partial shade.
Description A most attractive creeping plant with large, glossy, dark green leaves and tiny, white or pale pink flowers in July and August, followed by bright pink berries that last most of the winter.
Position In partial shade, but away from overhanging trees.
Propagation Strike cuttings of lateral shoots in late summer in a peat and sand mix. Overwinter in a cold frame and plant out the following spring.
Use The leaves have been used as a tea substitute; the oil is used to flavour toothpastes.
Others *Gaultheria shallon* is a similar plant that bears pale pink flowers earlier in the year, followed by black berries. The cowberry (*Vaccinium vitisidaea*) is another ground-cover plant with evergreen leaves and pink flowers followed by small red berries.

WOODRUFF
Asperula odorata (Rubiaceae)
Perennial. see page 80

Origins Europe, Siberia.
Ultimate size 6 × 18in (15 × 45cm).
Soil Light, moist.
Sun/shade Sun or partial shade.
Description An herbaceous plant that appears early in the spring, with whorls of bright green leaves on slender stems. In May and June, fragrant, white flowers appear at the tips of the stems.

Position An ideal plant for a wild garden, or to plant under the shade of trees where there is some moisture. It looks quite lovely planted near a patch of violets.

Propagation Lift a clump in the spring and divide the roots, replanting as required.

Use The scent of the leaves of woodruff – a sweet scent of new-mown hay – is apparent only when the leaves are dried. It is traditionally used to flavour German wine cups and was previously used as a strewing herb.

Others Dyer's woodruff (*Asperula tinctoria*) is very similar to woodruff, growing slightly taller with finer foliage. The white flowers follow later, in July.

YARROW

Achillea millefolium (Compositae)
Perennial.

Origins Temperate regions of Europe.

Ultimate size 1–3ft (30–90cm).
Soil Ordinary, moist.
Sun/shade Sun or light shade.
Description Feathery, deeply cut leaves are born on stems that are topped in summer and autumn by clusters of dirty white flowers.

Position Not a plant attractive enough to merit a prominent position, but, as its roots are claimed to secrete substances that help neighbouring plants to resist disease, its position should be chosen for horticultural and medicinal rather than decorative reasons.

Propagation Can be grown from seed or increased by division of the roots.

Use Chopped leaves added to the compost heap will hasten decomposition. Yarrow has long been used to heal wounds – try applying fresh leaves to small cuts.

Others *Achillea ptarmica*, sneezewort, is similar in appearance and use. *A. ptarmica* 'The Pearl' is a more attractive double-flowered variety, but the leaves are less aromatic.

HERBS FOR SPECIAL PURPOSES

Many people have very specific requirements when planting herbs in their gardens – the site may have particularly difficult soil, may be exposed to hot sun, may be very damp. Or it may be that colourful flowers are required to brighten up a dull corner, that the need is for fragrance, either of leaf or flower, or that the garden must provide materials for a flower arranger. We suggest here a wide range of herbs that may be useful in these and other situations. The lists are not, of course, exhaustive, but they include most of the commonly known herbs.

Herbs with Variegated Foliage

Golden
Balm, variegated lemon
Buxus elegantissima
Comfrey, dwarf
Elder, variegated
Honeysuckle, variegated
Marjoram, golden-tipped
Meadowsweet, variegated
Mint, ginger
Rue, variegated
Thyme 'Doone Valley'
Thyme, golden-lemon

Silver
Bugle, variegated
Comfrey, variegated
Figwort, variegated
Mint, pineapple
Thyme 'Silver Posie'

Multicoloured
Dock, bloody
Myrtle, variegated

Oleander, variegated
Orris, variegated
Sage, tricolour
Sweet flag, variegated

Herbs with Colourful Foliage

Silver
Alecost
Anthemis cupaniana
Artemisia pontica
Camphor
Catmint
Catsfoot
Costmary
Cotton lavender
Curry plant
Eucalyptus
Helichrysum
Horehound
Marsh mallow
Rosemary
Sage, Jerusalem
Santolina nana
S. neapolitana

S. serratifolia
Sea holly
Thistle, Scotch
Thyme, French
Thyme, 'Lanuginosus'
Thyme 'Silver Posie'
Thyme, silver-lemon
Wormwood 'Lambrook Silver'

Red/Bronze
Bugle, bronze
Elder, purple
Fennel, red
Lobelia cardinalis
Orach, red
Rosa rubrifolia
Salvia horminum

Yellow
Balm, golden
Bay, golden
Box, golden
Elder, cut-leaf golden
Elder, golden
Feverfew

Hop, golden
Meadowsweet, golden
Mint, ginger
Oregano, golden
Thyme 'E. B. Anderson'
Thyme, golden

Ground-cover Herbs

Ajuga
Balm, lemon
Bistort
Chamomile
Comfrey, dwarf
Creeping jenny
Meadowsweet
Mint
Oregano
Pennyroyal
Periwinkle
Pinks
Thrift
Thymes
Uva ursi
Wintergreen
Woodruff

Dye Plants

Alkanet
Bloodroot
Broom, dyer's
Chamomile, dyer's
Dandelion
Golden rod
Marigold
Madder
Ragwort
Safflower
Saffron
St John's wort
Tansy
Woad
Woodruff, dyer's

Herbs with Fragrant Leaves

Alecost
Angelica
Artemisia
Balm, lemon
Bergamot
Camphor
Catmint
Chamomile
Clary
Coriander
Curry plant
Dictamnus fraxinella
Geranium, scented
Hyssop
Lavender
Marjoram
Mint
Myrtle
Rosemary
Santolina
Sage
Savory
Southernwood
Sweet cicely
Thyme
Verbena, lemon

Herbs with Fragrant Flowers

Angelica
Bergamot
Chamomile
Cowslip
Daphne
Eglantine rose
Evening primrose
Heliotrope
Honeysuckle
Jasmine
Lavender
Lily of the valley
Pinks
Primrose
Rosemary
Mallow, musk
Myrtle
Sarcococca
Sweet rocket
Violet
Wallflower, wild
Witch hazel

Herbs for Flower Arrangers

Angelica
Bear's breech
Bergamot
Bistort
Columbine
Cornflower
Euphorbia
Foxglove
Fennel
Gayfeather
Gladwin
Lady's mantle
Lovage
Marigold, pot
Orach
Pinks
Poppies
Rue

Salvia
Santolina
Sweet cicely
Verbascum
Yarrow

Herbs for Formal Hedges

Box
Curry plant
Germander
Hyssop
Lavender
Rosemary
Rue
Santolina
Savory, winter
Southernwood
Yew

Herbs for Edging

Catmint
Chives
Lady's mantle
Marjoram
Parsley
Pinks
Savory, winter
Strawberry, alpine
Thrift
Thyme

Herbs with Colourful Flowers

Red
Bergamot
Lobelia cardinalis
Nasturtium
Pasque flower
Pinks
Poppies
Sage, pineapple
Salvia
Valerian

Pink
Bergamot
Bistort
Chives, Forcaste
Foxglove
Gayfeather
Germander
Hyssop
Mallow, marsh
Mallow, musk
Marjoram
Pinks
Queen of the meadow
Roses
Saffron
Salvia
Soapwort
Thrift
Thyme

Yellow
Arnica
Broom
Chamomile, dyer's
Cowslip
Elecampane
Evening primrose
Golden rod
Lady's mantle
Marigold
Mullein
Nasturtium
Safflower
Sage, Jerusalem
Sunflower
St John's wort
Tansy
Woad

Blue
Aconite
Borage
Bugle
Catmint
Chicory
Flax
Hyssop

Jacob's ladder
Lobelia
Rosemary
Salvia hispanica
S. patens

Purple
Bergamot
Chives
Columbine
Comfrey
Gayfeather
Heliotrope
Hyssop
Jacob's ladder
Lavender
Loosestrife, purple
Lungwort
Monkshood
Orris
Pasque flower
Rampion
Saffron
Sage, Russian
Salvia horminum
Scabious
Sweet rocket
Thistle, Scotch
Violet
Viper's bugloss

White
Bergamot
Chamomile
Evening primrose
Gayfeather
Hyssop
Jacob's ladder
Mallow, musk
Myrtle
Orris
Rosemary
Sneezewort
Sweet cicely
Sweet rocket
Woodruff
Yarrow

Herbs for Special Environments

Hot and Dry
Alecost
Calamint
Catmint
Curry plant
Euphorbia
Evening primrose
Fennel
Helichrysum
Horehound
Hyssop
Juniper
Lavender
Mullein
Nasturtium
Oregano
Pasque flower
Rosemary
Rue
Sage, Russian
Salvia
Savory, winter
Thistle, Scotch
Soapwort
Tarragon
Teucrium fruticans
Thrift
Thyme

Sun and Damp Soil
Aconite
Angelica
Bergamot
Burnet
Comfrey
Mace
Mallow, marsh
Self heal
Sneezewort

Dappled Shade
Aconite
Alkanet
Angelica

Bistort
Bugle
Burdock
Chervil
Feverfew
Foxglove
Hellebore
Jacob's ladder
Lady's mantle
Lungwort
Mallow, marsh
Mint
Monkshood
Primrose
Queen of the meadow
Sorrel
Strawberry
St John's wort
Sweet cicely
Valerian
Wintergreen

Dry Shade
Bugle
Comfrey
Foxglove
Honeysuckle
Lady's mantle
Periwinkle
Skirret
Solomon's seal
Valerian

Waterside and Bog
Bistort
Brooklime
Bogbean
Comfrey
Elecampane
Fern, royal
Figwort, water
Flag, sweet
Flag, yellow
Gayfeather
Loosestrife, purple
Mace
Mallow, marsh

Meadowsweet
Primula florindae
Soapwort
Sweet cicely
Valerian
Watercress
Watermint
Yarrow

Near the Sea
Balm, lemon
Bay
Bistort
Evening primrose
Pasque flower
Rosa rugosa
Rosemary
Rue
Salvia
Santolina
Sedum
Teucrium fruticans
Thrift

Herbs for Difficult Soils

Chalky Soil
Borage
Buddleia
Chamomile, dyer's
Chives
Fennel
Juniper
Mullein
Oregano
Pasque flower
Sage, Russian
Salvia
Scabious
Thyme
Toadflax
Wallflower, wild

Clay Soil
Comfrey
Elecampane
Geranium

Golden rod
Hellebore
Jacob's ladder
Lady's mantle
Queen of the meadow

Herbs for Pot-pourris

Alecost
Bergamot
Flag, sweet
Lavender
Rose, apothecary's
Rose, Rosa Mundi
Rosemary
Sage
Southernwood

Patio Herbs

Bay
Basil
Coriander
Geranium, scented
Marjoram
Nasturtium
Parsley
Rosemary, prostrate

Sage
Strawberry, alpine
Tarragon
Thyme
Violet
Woodruff

Culinary Herbs

For fish
Bay
Chervil
Dill
Fennel
Lovage
Parsley

For meats
Bay
Basil
Caraway
Chervil
Marjoram
Mints
Parsley
Rosemary
Sage
Savory, summer

Savory, winter
Tarragon
Thyme

For Salads
Bistort
Chives
Fennel
Hyssop
Lovage
Orach
Purslane
Savory, summer
Salad burnet
Sorrel
Sweet cicely

For egg dishes
Basil
Chervil
Chives
Coriander
Dill
Fennel
Savory, summer
Sorrel
Tarragon
Lemon thyme

For vegetables
Basil
Bay
Borage
Chervil
Chives
Dill
Fennel
Marjoram
Mint
Parsley
Rosemary
Sage
Savory, summer
Tarragon
Thyme

For fines herbes
Chervil
Chives
Parsley
Tarragon

For bouquet garni
Bay
Marjoram
Parsley
Thyme

SOCIETIES

Australia
The Herb Society of Western Australia
149 Bradford Street
Coolbinia
Western Australia   6050

Herb Society of North Queensland
P. O. Box 314
Paddington
Queensland   4814

The Herb Society of South Australia
P. O. Box 140
Park Side
South Australia   5063

The Tasmanian Herb Society
12 Delta Avenue
Taroona
Tasmania   7006

The Herb Society of Victoria
P. O. Box 2239
St Kilda West
Victoria   3182

New Zealand
Canterbury Herb Society
Mrs L. Thompson
3 McCorkindale
Christchurch

The Auckland Herb Society
P. O. Box 20 022
Glend Eden
Auckland

United Kingdom
The British Herb Trades Association
Jessica Houdret
Farnham Court
Church Road
Farnham Royal
Slough   SL2 3AW

The Herb Society
P.O. Box 415
London   SW1P 2HE

Midland Herb Society
c/o Hazel Paton
45 Solihull Road
Shirley
Solihull
West Midlands   B90 3HG

Lincolnshire Herb Society
c/o Brian Holman
45 Chestnut Road
North Hykeham
Lincoln   LN6 8LS

United States
The Herb Society of America, Inc.
9019 Kirtland Chardon Road
Mentor
Ohio 44060

International Herb Growers
    and Marketers Association
P.O. Box 281
Silver Springs
Pennsylvania 17575

GARDENS TO VISIT

British Isles

England
Avon
American Museum, Claverton Manor, Bath
Orchard House, Claverton, Bath

Berkshire
Hollington Herb Garden, Woolton Hill, Newbury
The Old Vicarage, Bucklebury
W. I. Education Centre, Denham College, near
    Abingdon

Buckinghamshire
Milton's Cottage, Dean Way, Chalfont St Giles

Cambridgeshire
Botanic Gardens, Cambridge
Emmanuel College, Cambridge
River Cam Farm House, Wimpole

Cheshire
Arley Hall and Gardens, near Northwich
Little Moreton Hall, Congleton

Cornwall
County Demonstration Garden, Probus

Cumbria
Acorn Bank Garden, Temple Sowerby, near Penrith
Dalemain, near Penrith

Derbyshire
Elvaston Castle, County Park, Borrowash Road,
    Elvaston

Haddon Hall, Bakewell
Hardwick Hall, Doe Lea, Chesterfield

Devon
Buckland Abbey, Yelverton
Castle Drogo, Drewsteignton
Fursdon House, Cadbury, Thorveton
Oldway Mansion Gardens, Paignton
The Old Barn, Fremington, Barnstaple

Dorset
Cranborne Manor Garden, Cranborne
Deans Court, Wimborne Minster
Highbury, near Wimborne
Red House Museum, Christchurch

Gloucestershire
Alderley Grange, Alderley, Wotton-
    under-Edge
Barnsley House Garden, Barnsley, near
    Cirencester
Hidcote Manor Garden, Hidcote Bartrim,
    Chipping Campden
Selsley Herb and Goat Farm, Selsley
Snowshill Manor, near Broadway
Sudeley Castle, Winchcombe
The Dower House, Badminton
Westbury Court, Westbury-on-Severn

Hampshire
Butser Ancient Farm Research Project, Rookham
    Lodge, East Meon
The Cloisters of Beaulieu Abbey

Curtis Museum & Allen Gallery, 10/12 Church
  Street, Alton
Holywell, Swanmore
Mechellmersh Court, Romsey
The Tudor Garden Museum, Bugle Street,
  Southampton
West Green House, Hartley Wintney

Hereford and Worcester
Abbey Dore Court Garden, near Hereford

Hertfordshire
Capel Manor, near Enfield
Hatfield House, Hatfield
Knebworth House, Knebworth
The Manor House, Chenies, Rickmansworth

Kent
Benenden Walled Garden, Benenden, Cranbrook
Hever Castle, Nr Edenbridge, Knole, Sevenoaks
Iden Croft Herbs, Frittenden Road, Staplehurst
Leeds Castle, near Maidstone
Marle Place, Brenchley
Scotney Castle Garden, Lamberhurst, Tunbridge
  Wells
Sissinghurst Castle Garden, Sissinghurst, near
  Cranbrook
Stoneacre, Stoneacre Lane, Offham, near
  Maidstone
Swanton Mill, Mersham
Withersdale Hall, near Ashford

Leicestershire
Manor House, Donington-le-Heath
Newarke House Museum, The Newarke, Leicester
Stone Cottage, Hambleton
University of Leicester Botanic Gardens,
  Beaumont Hall, Stoughton Drive South, Oadby

Lincolnshire
Gunby Hall, Burgh-le-Marsh

London
Chelsea Physic Garden, 66 Royal Hospital Road,
  SW3
Fulham Palace Gardens, Fulham
Hall Place, Bexley

Hampton Court Palace, Hampton Court
Museum of Garden History, St Mary-at-Lambeth,
  Lambeth
Westminster Abbey College Gardens, Westminster

Merseyside
The University of Liverpool Botanic Gardens,
  Ness, Norton, South Wirral

Norfolk
Felbrigg Hall, Norwich
Norfolk Lavender, Caley Mill, Heacham
Swannington Manor Gardens, Swannington, near
  Norfolk

Northamptonshire
Delapre Abbey, Northampton
Holdenby House Gardens, Holdenby,
  Northampton

Northumberland
Herterton House, Cambo

Nottinghamshire
Clumber Park, Worksop
Holme Pierrepont Hall, Radcliffe-on-Trent, near
  Nottingham
South Collingham House, Collingham

Oxfordshire
Cogges Farm Museum, Witney
Marndhill, Ardington, Troy, Ewelme
Waterperry Gardens, near Wheatley

Shropshire
Mawley Hall, Cleobury, Mortimer

Somerset
Combe Sydenham Hall, Monksilver
East Lambrook Manor, South Petherton
Gaulden Manor, Tollard, near Taunton

Staffordshire
Izaak Walton Cottage, Shallowford
Moseley Old Hall, Fordhouses, Wolverhampton

Suffolk
Gainsborough's House, Sudbury
Melford Hall, Long Melford, Sudbury
Netherfield Herbs, Rougham Green
The Priory, Lavenham
Thornham Manor Herb Garden, Thornham
    Magna

Surrey
The Herb Garden, The Queen's House, Kew
    Gardens
The Royal Horticultural Society's Garden, Wisley,
    Woking

Sussex (East)
Bateman's, Burwash
Michelham Priory, Upper Dicker, near Hailsham
Newick Park, Lewes

Sussex (West)
Clock House, Denmans, Fontwell, near Arundel
Cooke's House, West Burton
Fishbourne Roman Palace, Salthill Road,
    Fishbourne
Horsham Museum, 9 The Causeway, Horsham
Parham House and Gardens, Pulborough

Tyne and Wear
The Bede Monastery Museum, Jarrow Hall,
    Jarrow

Warwickshire
Anne Hathaway's Cottage, Shottery, Stratford-
    upon-Avon
New Place, Chapel Street, Stratford-upon-Avon
Queen's Park, Harborne, Birmingham

West Midlands
Selly Manor and Minworth Greaves, Sycamore
    Road, Bournville, Birmingham

Wiltshire
Avebury Manor, Avebury
Hillbarn House, Great Bedwyn

Yorkshire (North)
Perceval Hall Gardens, Burnsall

Yorkshire (West)
Abbey House Museum, Abbey Road, Leeds
East Riddlesden Hall, Bradford Road,
    Keighley
York Gate, Abel, Leeds

Ireland

Springhill, Springhill Road, Moneymore,
    Magheraft, County Londondery
Donaghmore House, Ballygarrett, Gorey, County
    Wexford

Scotland

Botanic Gardens, off Great Western Road,
    Glasgow
Earlshall Castle, Leuchars, Fife
The Edinburgh Botanic Gardens, Edinburgh
Netherbyres, near Eyemouth, Berwickshire
Priorwood Gardens, Melrose

Wales

Bible Garden, Bangor
Bryn Bras Castle, Llanrug, near Caernarfon,
    Gwynnedd
St Fagan's Garden, Cardiff

United States

Alabama
Popes Tavern Museum, 203 Hermitage Drive,
    Florence
The Orderman-Shaw House and Garden, 309
    North Hull Street, Montgomery

Arizona
Sharlot Hall Memorial Rose Garden, 415 West
    Gurley Street, Prescott
Tucson Botanical Gardens, 2150 North Alvernon,
    Tucson

Arkansas
Arkansas Territorial Restoration, 214 East Third
    Street, Little Rock

California
Los Angeles State and County Arboretum, W-301 North Baldwin Avenue, Arcadia
Rush Botanical Garden, 7801 Auburn Avenue, Citrus Heights
Fullerton Arboretum, California State University, Fullerton
J. Paul Getty Museum, 17985 Pacific Coast Highway, Malibu
Lakeside Park Garden Center, 666 Belleview Avenue, Oakland
Riverside Botanic Gardens, Main Campus, University of California, Riverside
The Huntington Botanical Gardens, 1151 Oxford Road, San Marino
Sarah May Downie Memorial Herb Garden, North Flower Street and North Park Boulevard, Santa Ana

Colorado
Botanic Gardens, 909 York Street, Denver

Connecticut
Capriland Herb Farm, Silver Street, Coventry
Scott-Fanton Museum Garden, 43 Main Street, Danbury
Bales-Schofield House, 45 Old Kings Highway, Darien
Thomas Lee House, Route 156, East Lyme
Pratt House, 20 West Avenue, Essex
Ogden House, 1520 Bronson Road, Fairfield
Stanley Whitman House, 37 High Street, Farmington
The Wilhemina Ann Arnold Barnhart Memorial Gardens, Hayden Hill Road, Haddam
Harriet Beecher Stowe House, 77 Forrest Street, Hartford
Hendricks Cottage Herb Garden, Simsbury Historic Centre, 800 Hopmeadow Street, Simsbury
Webb-Deane-Stevens Museum, Main Street, Wethersfield

Delaware
Corbit-Sharp House, 2nd and Main Streets, Odessa
The Homestead, Doods Lane, Rehoboth Beach

District of Columbia
Bishop's Garden, Washington Cathedral Grounds, Massachusetts and Wisconsin Avenues, Washington
United States National Arboretum, 24 and R Streets NE, Washington

Florida
Four Arts Garden, Four Arts Plaza, Royal Palm Way, Palm Beach

Georgia
Atlanta Botanical Garden, Piedmont Park, Piedmont Drive, Atlanta
Atlanta Historical Society Grounds, 3101 Andrews Drive NW, Atlanta

Illinois
Marquette Park Rose and Trial Gardens, 3540 W 71st Street, Chicago
Dr Fifthian Herb Garden, Vermillion County Museum, 115 N Gilbert Street, Danville
Lake of the Wood Botanic Garden, Early American Museum, Mahomet
Glen Oak Botanical Garden, Prospect and McClure Avenues, Peoria

Indiana
Huntington College Arboretum and Botanical Garden, Upper Wabash Basin National Research Center, 2303 College Avenue, Huntington
Dr William Hutchings Medicinal Herb Garden, 120 W 3rd Street, Madison

Kentucky
Ashland Henry Clay Mansion, E Main Street and Sycamore, Lexington
Farmington Historic House Museum, 3033 Bardstown Road, Louisville

Louisiana
American Rose Society Garden, Jefferson-Paige Road, Shreveport
Rosedown Plantation and Gardens, US 61 and Route 10, St Francisville

Maine
Henry Wadsworth Longfellow Home, 487
    Congress Street, Portland

Maryland
National Colonial Farm, Bryan Point Road,
    Accokeek
Cylburn Wild Flower Preserve and Garden Center,
    Cylburn Park, 4915 Greensprings Avenue,
    Baltimore
London Town Publik House and Gardens, 839
    London Town Road, Edgewater
Hampton House Gardens, 535 Hampton Lane,
    Towson

Massachusetts
Shaker Village, Hancock
John Whipple House, 53 S Main Street, Ipswich
Heritage Plantation, Grove and Pine Streets,
    Sandwich
Berkshire Garden Center, junction of Routes 102
    and 183, Stockbridge
Old Sturbridge Village, Routes 15 and 20,
    Sturbridge

Michigan
Matthaei Botanical Gardens, University of
    Michigan, 1800 Dixboro Road, Ann Arbor
Fernwood Botanic Garden and Nature Center,
    1720 Range Line Road, Niles

Missouri
Missouri Botanical Gardens, 2101 Tower Grove
    Avenue, St Louis

Nebraska
Chet Ager Nature Center, Van Dorn and SW 40th
    Streets, Lincoln

New Hampshire
Pierce Manse, 14 Penacook Street, Concord
Strawbery Bank, Old South End, Portsmouth

New Jersey
Deep Cut Park Horticultural Center, Newman
    Springs Road, Middletown
18th-century Herb Garden, Marlpit Hall, Kings
    Highway, Middletown

Israel Crane House, 110 Orange Road, Montclair
The Force House Herb Garden, South Livingston
    Avenue, Livingston
Allen House, Shrewsbury
Reeves-Reed Arboretum, 165 Hobart Avenue,
    Summit

New York
Sagtikos Manor, Montauk Highway, Bay Shore
Boscobel Restoration, Route 9D, Garrison-on-
    Hudson
The Cornell Plantation, 100 Judd Falls Road,
    Ithaca
Johnson Hall, Hall Avenue, Johnstown
John Jay Homestead, John Jay Street, Katonah
General Herkimer Home State Historical Site,
    Little Falls
Old Westbury Gardens, 71 Old Westbury Road,
    Long Island
Brooklyn Botanic Garden, 1000 Washington
    Avenue, New York City
The Cloisters, Metropolitan Museum, Fort Tryon
    Park, Manhattan, New York City
New York Botanical Garden, Bronx Park, E 200th
    Street, New York City
Queens' Botanical Garden, 42–50 Main Street
    Flushing, New York City
Staten Island Botanical Garden, 914 Richmond
    Terrace, New York City
Van Cortland Mansion Museum, Van Cortland
    Park, Broadway and 246 Street, New York City
Wave Hill, 675 W 252 Street, New York City
Museum of Arts and Science, 687 East Avenue,
    Rochester
Robison Herb Garden, Union College Campus,
    Nott Street, Schenectady

North Carolina
University Botanical Gardens, University of North
    Carolina, Weaver Boulevard, Asheville
North Carolina Botanical Garden, University of
    North Carolina, Totten Center, Laurel Hill
    Road, Chapel Hill
Haywood Horticultural Gardens, Haywood
    Technical College, Freedlander Drive, Clyde
Elizabethan Gardens, Fort Raleigh National
    Historic Site, Manteo

Ohio

The Western Reserve Herb Society Garden, The Garden Center of Greater Cleveland, 11030 East Boulevard, Cleveland

George P. Crosby Gardens, 2518 Morgan Road, Toledo

Inniswood Botanical Garden and Nature Preserve, 940 Hempstead Road, Westerville

Oregon

Mount Pisgah Arboretum, Mount Pisgah Road, Eugene

Pennsylvania

Old Economy Gardens, Route 65, Ambridge

Delaware Valley College, Route 202 and New Britain Road, Doylestown, Philadelphia

Longwood Gardens, Kennett Square, Philadelphia

Phipps Conservatory, Schenley Park, Pittsburgh

Rhode Island

Old Slater Mill Museum Fiber and Dye Garden, Roosevelt and Main Streets, Pawtucket

South Carolina

Magnolia Plantations and Garden, Ashley River Road, Charleston

Clemson University Horticultural Gardens, Clemson University, Clemson

South Dakota

McCrory Gardens, South Dakota State University, Route 14-E, Brookings

Tennessee

All-American Trial Gardens, University of Tennessee, Neyland Drive, Knoxville

Mageveny House, 198 Adams Avenue, Memphis

Tennessee Botanical Gardens and Fine Arts Center, Forrest Park Drive, Nashville

Texas

Valley Botanical Garden, Route 83, McAllen

Hilltop Herb Farm, Route 1725, Cleveland

The Houston Arboretum and Botanical Society, 4501 Woodway Drive, Houston

San Antonio Botanical Center, 555 Funston Place, San Antonio

Vermont

Stone Chimney Gardens, Reading

Shelburne Museum Garden, Route 7, Shelburne

Virginia

Orland E. White Arboretum, University of Virginia, Route 50, Boyce

Belle Air Plantation, Route 5, Charles City

Mary Washington House and Garden, Charles and Lewis Streets, Fredericksburg

Mount Vernon, Mount Vernon Memorial Highway, Mount Vernon

Wisconsin

Alfred L. Boerner Botanical Gardens, 5879 S 92nd Street, Hales Corner

Paine Art Center and Arboretum, 1410 Algoma Road, Oshkosh

BIBLIOGRAPHY

Anderson, Anne, *Herbs of Long Ago – Canadian Indians*, University of Alberta Press, Edmonton, 1982

Bacon, Richard M., *The Forgotten Arts: Growing, Gardening, and Cooking with Herbs*, Yankee Publishing Inc., Dublin, New Hampshire, 1972

Bardswell, Francesca, *The Herb Garden*, Adam & Charles Black, London, 1911

The Beginner's Herb Garden, Herb Society of America, Inc., Mentor, Ohio, 1983

Bonar, Ann, *The Macmillan Treasury of Herbs*, Macmillan Publishing Company, Inc., New York, 1985

Bown, Deni, *Fine Herbs: Fine Herbs for a Beautiful Garden*, Unwin Hyman Ltd, London, 1988

Boxer, Arabella, & Back, Philippa, *The Herb Book*, Octopus, London, 1974

Bremness, Lesley, *The Complete Book of Herbs*, Dorling Kindersley, London, 1988

Brownlow, Margaret, *Herbs and The Fragrant Garden*, The Herb Farm Limited, 1957

Clarkson, Rosetta E., *Herbs: their Culture and Uses*, Macmillan, London, 1961

Clarkson, Rosetta E., *The Golden Age of Herbs and Herbals*, Constable, London, 1973

Davies, Jill, *Herbs and Herb Gardens*, Shire Publications, Aylesbury, 1983

Foster, Steven, *Herbal Bounty: The Gentle Art of Herb Cultivation*, Smith, Gibbs, Publishing, Layton, Utah, 1984

Fox, Helen M., *Gardening with Herbs for Flavor and Fragrance*, Dover Publications, Inc., New York, 1972

Garland, Sarah, *The Herb Garden*, Windward, Leicester, 1984

Grieve, M., *A Modern Herbal*, Jonathan Cape, London, 1931

Griffiths, Trevor, *The Book of Old Roses*, Michael Joseph, London, 1984

Grigson, Geoffrey, *A Herbal of All Sorts*, Phoenix House, London, 1959

Hall, Dorothy, *The Book of Herbs*, Angus & Robertson, London, 1972

Harvey, John, *Medieval Gardens*, B.T. Batsford Ltd, London, 1981

Hatfield, Audrey Wynne, *Pleasures of Herbs*, Museum Press Ltd, London, 1964

Hayes, Elizabeth, *Herbs, Flavours, and Spices*, Faber & Faber, London, 1961

Heath, Ambrose, *Herbs in the Kitchen*, Faber & Faber, London, 1953

Hewer, D.G., *Practical Herb Growing*, G. Bell & Sons Ltd, London, 1946

H.M.S.O., *Culinary and Medicinal Herbs*, London, 1951

Hogner, Dorothy Childs, *Herbs from the Garden to the Table*, Oxford University Press, New York, 1953

Hopkinson, S. and J., *The Hollington Manual*, Hollington Herbs, Newbury, 1983

Kadans, Joseph, *Modern Encyclopedia of Herbs*, Prentice Hall Press, Old Tappan, New Jersey, 1970

Kamm, Minnie W., *Old Time Herbs for Northern Gardens*, Dover Publications, Inc., New York, 1971

Leyel, C. F., *The Magic of Herbs*, Jonathan Cape, London, 1926

Leyel, C. F., *Herbal Delights*, Faber & Faber, London, 1937

Leyel, C. F., *Compassionate Herbs*, Faber & Faber, London, 1956

Leyel, C. F., *Heartsease*, Faber & Faber, London, 1959

Loewenfeld, Claire, *Herb Gardening: Why and How to Grow Herbs*, Faber & Faber, London, 1964

Loewenfeld, Claire, and Back, Philippa, *The Complete Book of Herbs and Spices*, David & Charles, Newton Abbot, 1978

Lust, John (ed), *The Herb Book*, Bantam Books, Inc., New York, 1983

Mabey, Richard, *Plants with a Purpose*, Collins, London, 1977

Mabey, Richard (ed), *The Complete New Herbal*, Elm Tree Books, London, 1988

Macleod, Dawn, *A Book of Herbs*, Gerald Duckworth & Co., Ltd, London, 1968

Macleod, Dawn, *Popular Herbs: their History, Growth, and Use*, Gerald Duckworth & Co., Ltd, London, 1981. Distributed in the United States of America by Longwood Publishing Group, Inc., Wolfeboro, New Hampshire.

Macleod, Dawn, *Down to Earth Women*, William Blackwood, London, 1982

Paterson, Allen, *Herbs in The Garden*, J. M. Dent & Sons Ltd, London, 1985

Ranson, Florence, *British Herbs*, Penguin Books, London, 1949

Reid, Shirley, *Herbs for the Home and Garden*, Salem House Publications/Angus and Robertson, Topsfield, Massachusetts/North Ryde, New South Wales, 1988

Rohde, Eleanour Sinclair, *A Garden of Herbs*, The Medici Society, London, 1921

Rohde, Eleanour Sinclair, *Herbs and Herb Gardening*, The Medici Society, London, 1936

Sanecki, Kay N., *The Book of Herbs*, Magna Books, Leicester, 1984

Simmons, Adelma G., *Herb Gardens of Delight*, Clinton Press, New York, 1974

Sitton, Diane M., *Texas Gardener's Guide to Growing and Using Herbs*, Texas Gardener Press, Waco, Texas, 1987. Distributed by Texas Monthly Press, Austin, Texas.

Stuart, M., *The Encyclopedia of Herbs and Herbalism*, Orbis Publishing, London, 1979

Sunset editors, *Herbs: How to Grow*, Sunset Books/Lane Publishing Company, Menlo Park, California, 1972

Szekely, Edmond B., *The Book of Herbs*, I.B.S. Internacional, San Diego, California, 1981

Tomikel, John, *Edible Wild Plants and Useful Herbs*, Allegheny Press, Elgin, Pennsylvania, 1986

Zabar, Abbie, *The Potted Herb*, Stewart, Tabori, & Chang, Inc., New York, 1988

INDEX OF BOTANICAL NAMES

Every much-used herb has beome known by a number of common, popular, often local names, so that even in the same country, much less across national boundaries, the same herb may masquerade under a variety of names. Here we list the herbs under their Latin names and give their most frequently used American and British popular names. The name in the last column is that under which the herb is listed in A Selection of Garden Herbs.

Botanical name	American	British	
Achillea millefolium	Yarrow, Sneezewort, Nosebleed, Milfoil	Yarrow, Sneezewort, Devil's nettle, Old man's pepper	Yarrow
Agastache anethiodora	Anise hyssop, Licorice mint	Anise hyssop	Anise hyssop
Alchemilla vulgaris	Lady's mantle	Lady's mantle, Lion's foot	Lady's mantle
Allium schoenoprasum	Chives, Onion	Chives	Chives
Aloysia triphylla	Lemon verbena	Lemon verbena	Lemon verbena
Anethum graveoloens	Dill	Dill, Dilly	Dill
Angelica archangelica	European angelica, The root of the Holy Ghost	Angelica	Angelica
Anthemis nobilis flore pleno	Double-flowered chamomile, Ground apple	Double-flowered chamomile	Chamomile, double-flowered
Anthemis tinctoria	Golden marguerite	Dyer's chamomile	Chamomile, dyer's
Anthriscus cerefolium	Chervil	Chervil	Chervil
Artemisia abrotanum	Southernwood, Lad's love	Southernwood, Old man, Lad's love	Southernwood
A. dracunculus	Estragon, French tarragon	Tarragon, Little dragon	Tarragon, French
Asperula odorata	Master of the wood, Sweet woodruff	Woodruff, Sweet woodruff	Woodruff
Atriplex hortensis 'Ruba'	Garden orach	Red orach, Arrach, Mountain spinach	Orach, red
Balsamita vulgaris 'Tomentosum'	Camphor	Camphor plant	Camphor
Borago officinalis	Borage	Borage, Bugloss, Burrage	Borage

Botanical name	American	British	
Buxus sempervirens	Boxwood, Bush tree	Box	Box
Calendula officinalis	Calendula, Mary Bud	Pot marigold, Hens and chickens	Marigold, pot
Coriandrum sativum	Coriander, Cilandro	Coriander, Chinese parsley	Coriander
Dianthus caesius	Pink	Cheddar pink	Pink, Cheddar
Digitalis lutea	Yellow foxglove	Yellow foxglove	Foxglove, yellow
D. purpurea	American foxglove	Foxglove, Dead men's bells	Foxglove
Dipsacus fullonum	Teasel	Teasel	Teasel
Echium vulgare	Blue devil, Blue weed	Viper's bugloss	Viper's bugloss
Eruca sativa	Rocket	Rocket	Rocket
Eupatorium purpureum	Queen of the meadow, Joe Pye weed, Sweet Joe Pye	Queen of the meadow, Gravelroot	Queen of the meadow
Foeniculum vulgare 'Purpureum'	Red fennel	Bronze fennel	Fennel, bronze
Fragaria vesca	Wood strawberry	Alpine strawberry	Strawberry, alpine
Galega officinalis 'Alba'	White goat's rue	White goat's rue	Goat's rue, white
Gaultheria procumbens	Checkerberry, Mountain tea, Spiceberry	Wintergreen, Checkerberry, Partridge berry	Wintergreen
Geranium macrorrhizum	Cranesbill	Cranesbill	Cranesbill
Helichrysum angustifolium	Curry plant, White leaf everlasting	Curry plant	Curry plant
Hesperis matronalis	Sweet rocket	Sweet rocket, Dame's rocket	Sweet rocket
Humulus lupulus 'Aureus'	Hop bine, whitebine	Golden hop	Hop, golden
Hyssopus aristatus	Dwarf hyssop	Rock hyssop	Hyssop, rock
H. officinalis 'Roseus'	Pink hyssop	Pink hyssop	Hyssop, pink
Inula helenium	Elecampane, Elfdock, Horseheal, Scabwort	Elecampane, Elfwort, Velvet dock	Elecampane
Iris germanica	Orris root	Orris	Orris
Laurus nobilis	Bay laurel, Laurel, Roman laurel	Bay, Sweet bay	Bay
Lavandula angustifolia 'Hidcote'	Hidcote lavender	Hidcote lavender	Lavender 'Hidcote'
L. latifolia 'Loddon Pink'	Loddon Pink lavender	Loddon Pink lavender	Lavender 'Loddon Pink'
Levisticum officinale	European lovage, Maggi plant, Sea parsley	Lovage	Lovage
Lonicera × americana	Honeysuckle	American honeysuckle	Honeysuckle, American
Lythrum salicaria	Loosestrife, Long purple, Spiked loosestrife	Purple loosestrife	Loosestrife, purple
Malva moschata 'Alba'	White mallow	White musk mallow	Mallow, white musk
Melissa officinalis 'Variegata'	Bee balm, Sweet balm	Variegated lemon balm	Lemon balm, variegated

Botanical name	American	British	
Mentha × piperita nm. 'Citrata'	Orange mint, Perfume mint	Eau-de-Cologne mint	Mint, eau-de-Cologne
M. rotundifolia 'Variegata'	Pineapple mint	Pineapple mint, Variegated apple mint	Mint, pineapple
M. spicata	Lamb mint, Sage of Bethlehem, Spearmint	Garden mint, Spearmint	Mint, garden
Monarda didyma	Bee balm, High balm, Mountain balm, Oswego tea	Bergamot	Bergamot
Myrrhis odorata	Anise root, Garden myrrh, Sweet chervil	Sweet cicely	Sweet cicely
Nepeta mussini	Catnip	Catmint	Catmint
Ocimum basilicum	Basil, Sweet basil	Basil, Sweet basil, St Josephwort	Basil
Oenothera biennis	Evening primrose, Fever plant, King's cureall	Evening primrose, Evening star	Evening primrose
Origanum majorana	Marjoram, Sweet marjoram	Marjoram, Sweet marjoram, Knotted marjoram	Marjoram, sweet
O. vulgare 'Aureum'	Golden oregano	Golden marjoram, Golden oregano	Marjoram, golden
O. v. 'Compactum'	Trailing oregano	Compact marjoram	Marjoram, compact
Papaver commutatum 'Ladybird'	Ladybird poppy	Ladybird poppy	Poppy 'Ladybird'
Pelargonium graveolens	Rose geranium	Rose geranium	Geranium, rose
P. 'Lady Plymouth'	Lady Plymouth geranium	Lady Plymouth geranium	Geranium 'Lady Plymouth'
Petroselinum crispum	Curly parsley, Garden parsley, Rock parsley	Parsley	Parsley
Phytolacca americana	Inkberry, Pigeonberry, Pokeweed	Pokeroot	Pokeroot
Portulaca oleracea	Purslane	Purslane	Purslane
Primula veris	Cowslip	Cowslip, Paigles	Cowslip
R. eglantaria (syn. *R rubiginosa*)	Eglantine rose	Eglantine rose, Sweet brier	Rose, eglantine
Rosa gallica 'Officinalis'	French rose	Apothecary's rose	Rose, apothecary's
R.g. 'Versicolor'	Rosa Mundi	Rosa Mundi	Rosa Mundi
Rosmarinus officinalis	Rosemary	Rosemary, Compass plant	Rosemary
Rumex scutatus	French sorrel	Sorrel, Cuckoo sorrel	Sorrel
Ruta graveolens 'Jackman's Blue'	Common rue, German rue	Herb of Grace	Rue 'Jackman's Blue'
Salvia glutinosa			*Salvia glutinosa*
S. officinalis	Garden sage	Sage	Sage
S. o. 'Purpurascens'	Red sage, Purple sage	Purple sage, red sage	Sage, purple
S. rutilans		Pineapple sage	Sage, pineapple

Botanical name	American	British	
Sambucus nigra 'Purpurea'	Bronze elder	Purple elder	Elder, purple
Santolina chamaecyparissus	Lavender cotton	Cotton lavender, French lavender	Cotton lavender
S. viridis	Green santolina		Santolina, green
Satureja hortensis	Summer savory, Bean herb	Summer savory	Savory, summer
S. montana	Winter savory	Winter savory	Savory, winter
S. repandra	Creeping savory	Creeping savory	Savory, creeping
Symphytum grandiflorum	Dwarf comfrey	Boneset, Dwarf comfrey	Comfrey, dwarf
Teucrium chamaedrys	Germander	Wall germander, Horsechire	Germander
Thymus 'Doone Valley			Thyme 'Doone Valley'
T. serpyllum 'Coccineus'	Crimson thyme	Coccineus thyme	Thyme, crimson
T. vulgaris	English thyme, Garden thyme	Common thyme	Thyme
T. v. 'Silver Posie			Thyme 'Silver Posie'
Tropaeolum majus 'Alaska'	Indian cress, Variegated garden nasturtium	Variegated nasturtium	Nasturtium, variegated
Valeriana officinalis	Valerian, All-heal, Garden heliotrope, Fragrant valerian	Phu, Valerian, All-heal	Valerian
Viola odorata	English violet, Garden violet	Sweet violet	Violet
V. tricolor	Johnny Jumper, Pansy, Stepmother	Heartsease, Johnny-Jump-Up	Heartsease

INDEX

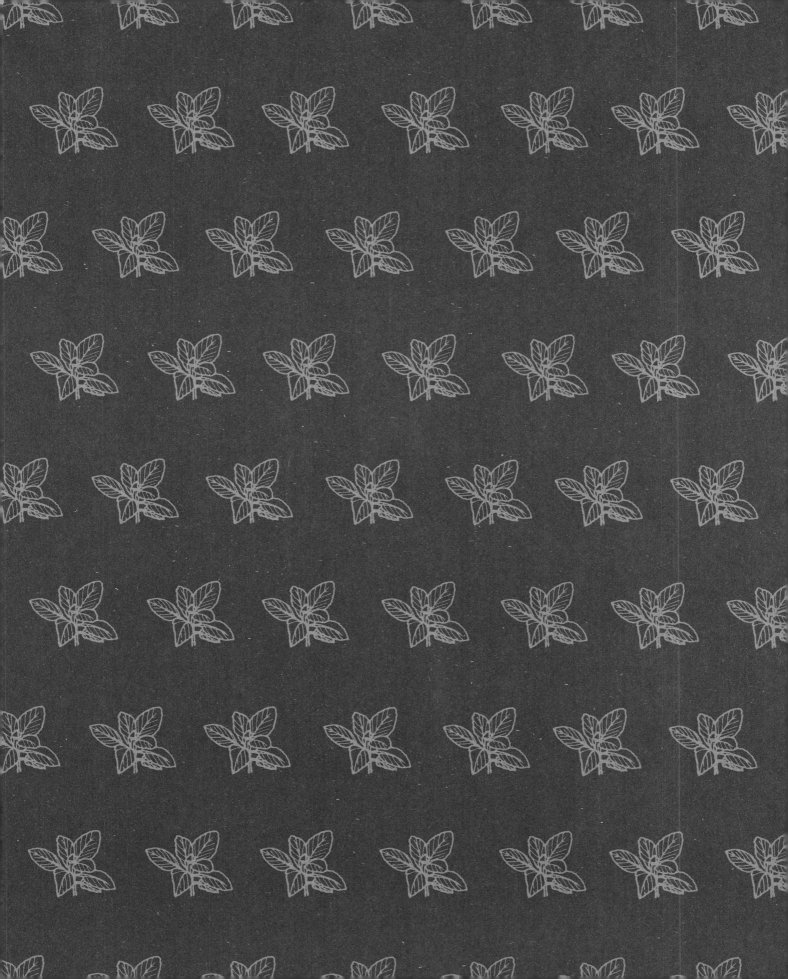